The Indians
of the Subarctic

BIBLIOGRAPHICAL SERIES

The Newberry Library Center
for the History of the American Indian

General Editors
Francis Jennings
Martin Zanger
Staff Editor
Joseph Narun

The Center is Supported by Grants from
The National Endowment for the Humanities
The Ford Foundation
The W. Clement and Jessie V. Stone Foundation
The Woods Charitable Fund, Inc.

The Indians
of the Subarctic

A Critical Bibliography

JUNE HELM

Published for the Newberry Library

Indiana University Press

BLOOMINGTON AND LONDON

Published in Canada by Fitzhenry & Whiteside Limited, Don Mills,
Ontario
Manufactured in the United States of America

Library of Congress Cataloging in Publication Data
Helm, June (formerly June Helm MacNeish) 1924–
The Indians of the subarctic.
(The Newberry Library Center for the History of
the American Indian bibliographical series)
1. Athapascan Indians—Bibliography. 2. Algon-
quian Indians—Bibliography. 3. Indians of North
America—Canada—Bibliography. 4. Indians of
North America—Alaska—Bibliography. I. Title.
II. Series: Newberry Library, Chicago. Center for
the History of the American Indian. The Newberry
Library Center for the History of the American
Indian bibliographical series.
Z1210.A75M33 1976 [E99.A86] 016.97'0004'97
76–12373
ISBN 0–253–33004–1 1 2 3 4 5 80 79 78 77 76

The Editors to the Reader

A massive literature exists for the history and culture of American Indians, but the quality of that literature is very uneven. At its best it compares well with the finest scholarship and most interesting reading to be found anywhere. At its worst it may take the form of malicious fabrication. Sometimes, well-intentioned writers give false impressions of reality either because of their own limitations of mind or because they lack adequate information. The consequence is a kind of chaos through which advanced scholars as well as new students must warily pick their way. It is, after all, a history of hundreds, if not thousands, of human communities spread over an entire continent and enduring through millenia of pre-Columbian years as well as the five centuries that Europeans have documented since 1492. That is not a small amount of history.

Often, however, historians have been so concerned with the affairs of European colonies or the United States that they have almost omitted Indians from their own history. "Frontier history" and the "history of Indian–White relations" frequently focus upon the intentions and desires of Euramericans, treating Native Americans as though they were merely natural parts of the landscape, like forests, or mountains, or wild animals — obstacles to "progress" or "civilization." One of the major purposes of the Newberry Library's Center for the History of the American Indian is to modify that narrow conception; to put Indians properly back into the central role in their own history and into the history of the United States of America as well — as participants in, rather than obstacles to, the creation of American society and culture.

The series of bibliographies, of which this book is one part, is intended as a guide to reliable sources and studies in particular fields of the general literature. Some of these are devoted to culture areas; others treat selected individual tribes; and a third group will speak to significant contemporary and historical issues.

The present volume is a strong reminder that culture areas exist in their own right, sprawling about with little regard to national or tribal territories; and we are further reminded that the range of culture includes more than survival traits, even though conditions may be such that survival can never be taken for granted. The Indians of the Subarctic have adapted to a physical habitat that imposes taxation in terms of time and energy far beyond the demands of most national governments, but they have preserved universal human qualities of thought and feeling as they found their particular species niche in the natural habitat. Ethnology here must stay within the narrow bounds set by ecology, yet even within so strict a compass there is variation and imagination.

This work is designed in a format, uniform throughout the entire series, to be useful to both beginning students and advanced scholars. It has two main parts: the essay (conveniently organized by subheadings) and an alphabetical list of all works cited. All citations in the essay are directly keyed, by means of bracketed numbers, to the more complete information in the list. In addition, the series incorporates several information-at-a-glance features. Preceding the list will be found two sets of recommended titles. One of these is a list of five items for the beginner; the second, a group of volumes that constitute a basic library collection in the field. Finally, asterisks within the alphabetical list denote works suitable for secondary school students. This apparatus has been built-in because the bibliographical essay, in a form familiar to scholars, will probably prove fairly hard going for beginners who may wish to put it aside until they have gained sufficient background from introductory materials. Such students should come back to the essay eventually, however, because it surveys a vast sweep of information about a great variety of persons, places, communities, and events.

There is variety also in the kinds of sources because these critical bibliographies support the study of ethnohistory. Unlike older, more narrow disciplines, ethnohistory embraces the entire culture of a people; it demands contributions from a wide range of source materials. Not the least of these in the history of American Indians are their own music, crafts, linguistics, and oral traditions. Whenever possible, the authors have included such sources as well as those associated with politics, economics, geography, and so on.

In the last analysis this work, like all other bibliographical devices, is a tool. Each author is an expert who knows the literature and advises what source is most helpful for which purpose, but students must use this help according to their individual purposes and capacities. Many ways suggest themselves. The decision is the reader's own.

Introduction*

Ethnologists concerned with the native peoples of
Subarctic North America often share the distress experienced by the author: generally, to even the educated
Canadian or American layman, "the North" means "Eskimo." No matter how firmly the researcher states the
Indian heritage of the peoples under study, he is apt to
be introduced as "So-and-so, who will tell you about his
work with the Eskimos." Furthermore, to the residents of
the continental United States, "the North" is limited to
"Alaska." It therefore seems appropriate to emphasize at
the outset that (a) most of the North American Subarctic
and its indigenous peoples are found within Canadian
territory; and (b) by far the greatest mass of the continental "North" — the land above the 55th parallel (and a
substantial portion of land in the eastern half of Canada

*Without the compilation of Athapaskan sources and materials
made possible by National Science Foundation grant GS–3057, I
would not have had the temerity to undertake this essay. Preparation
has been further eased by the annotated bibliographies that follow
each chapter of Graburn and Strong's *Circumpolar Peoples* [74] and by
Edward S. Roger's forthcoming "History of Ethnological Research in
the Shield Subarctic" [217]. For these aids, my thanks to the authors.
C. Douglas Ellis, Beryl C. Gillespie, Nelson H. H. Graburn, Margaret
Lantis, Catharine McClellan, Edward S. Rogers, B. Stephen Strong,
and James W. VanStone have responded to my request for a critical
reading of the draft. Improvements redound to their credit; deficien-
cies remain my own responsibility.

Margaret T. Hotopp prepared bibliography slips and mobilized
the resources of the University of Iowa Library and Inter-Library
Loan on my behalf; Pat Sadler joined her in the final phase. And, as
always, I appreciate Sheryl Schuder's meticulous typing of a difficult
manuscript.

between the 50th and 55th) — is inhabited by Algon-
quian- and Athapaskan-speaking Indians.* Their habitat
is the broad belt of boreal or northern coniferous forest
found in those latitudes, that great Hudsonian biotic
province of moose, caribou, black bear, and snowshoe
hare. The Eskimo or Inuit peoples are generally restricted to the coastal rim of the continent and the Arctic
islands. The interior barrengrounds or tundra between
the coast and the forest was aboriginally a buffer zone: in
a few areas Indians coming out to hunt the migratory
caribou beyond the edge of the woods might encounter
Eskimo moving inland for the same purpose. In the
public imagination, the glamour of the Arctic Eskimo,
surviving on the windswept coasts and polar ice pack, has
tended to obscure recognition of the hardihood and
effective adaptation of the Subarctic Indian who, with
snowshoe, toboggan, snare, bow and arrow, spear, and
fish net, has also for untold centuries wrested sustenance
from the harsh land.

Two recent publications offer surveys of peoples of
Subarctic North America. In *Circumpolar Peoples: An
Anthropological Perspective,* Nelson H. H. Graburn and B.
Stephen Strong [74] surveyed the entire Arctic and Sub-
arctic zones in which selected tribal groups within Sub-
arctic North America are spotlighted. James VanStone's

*The designation of lands above the 55th parallel breaks down on
the west coast of North America where the Pacific coast climate and
the ethnographic culture area of the Northwest Coast extend to about
the 60th parallel.

Athapaskan Adaptations [258] emphasizes the environmental adaptation of the Indians of the western sector of Subarctic North America.

Basic Reference Works: Identifications and Classifications

The forthcoming Volume VI of the *Handbook of North American Indians* series, *The Subarctic* edited by June Helm [91] has chapters on all tribal groups of the Subarctic and provides some degree of coverage of all the topics treated in this essay.* John R. Swanton's volume on *The Indian Tribes of North America* [242] contains entries on all Subarctic groups and emphasizes basic data such as location, alternate names and spellings, and population. Much of Swanton's material is derived from the tribal entries in the original two-volume *Handbook of American Indians North of Mexico* edited by Frederick Webb Hodge [101], which for half a century has remained the basic reference work for synonymies and succinct tribal histories. The brevity of the chapters on the Subarctic Indians in Diamond Jenness's *Indians of Canada* [119] is deceptive. Jenness's cultural and historical summaries are based on extensive and meticulous documentary research. *Alaska Natives and the Land* prepared by the United States Federal Field Committee for Development Planning in

*The terms "tribe" and "tribal" carry false implications of cultural, social, and political boundedness and centricity when applied to the native peoples of the Subarctic, but the English language provides no better term (unless one prefers the overly vague "group") to meet the scientist's need to lump and classify and thereby reduce a welter of variation and ambiguity to manageable units.

Alaska [253] is a compilation of basic data on the native peoples of Alaska, including many maps and much information on past and present village and tribal locations, resources, environmental zones, and recent economic conditions.

The sources cited above offer definitions and designations of tribal–dialectic groups and their boundaries and of subareal cultural groupings, accompanied by maps. Other works concerned with questions of identification, classification, and location include Jacob Fried's "A Survey of the Aboriginal Populations of Quebec and Labrador" [65]; Gontran Laviolette's three articles, "Notes on the Aborigines of the Province of Quebec" [138], "Notes on the Aborigines of the Province of Ontario" [140], and "Notes on the Aborigines of the Prairie Provinces" [139]; and Cornelius Osgood's *The Distribution of the Northern Athapaskan Indians* [184]. Harold E. Driver's *Indians of North America* [46] and Alfred L. Kroeber's *Cultural and Natural Areas of Native North America* [132] include Subarctic peoples in their coverage of all the native populations of North America.

The several efforts to demarcate cultural–areal subdivisions within the Subarctic have involved differential weighting of the criterion of language *vis-à-vis* general cultural correspondences and contrasts. The indigenous peoples of the American Subarctic are either of the Algonquian or of the Athapaskan language family, the boundary between these two great linguistic divisions occurring along a line extending west from the west side

of Hudson Bay. For present purposes, we may subdivide
the Subarctic culture area from east to west into: the
Subarctic Algonquians of the Canadian Shield; the
Athapaskans of the Shield and Mackenzie Lowlands;
the Cordilleran Athapaskans of northern British Columbia, the Yukon Territory, and eastern Alaska; the
Alaskan Athapaskans of the plateaus of the Yukon, Kuskokwim, and Tanana rivers; and the Athapaskans south
of the Alaska Range.

Another people of native ancestry must also be
recognized: the Métis, of mixed European and Indian
heritage, who are found in the northern portion of the
prairie provinces (Manitoba, Saskatchewan, Alberta) of
Canada and along the length of the Mackenzie River in
the Northwest Territories. The origins of this socially
and culturally intermediary population lie in the Red
River drainage of Manitoba. This essay treats only of
those descendants of the Red River Métis who moved
with the fur trade into the boreal forest of the Subarctic
and of those more recent Métis people of Anglo-
Athapaskan extraction in the lower Mackenzie region.

Major Ethnographies

Certain monographs on the peoples of the Subarctic
may be considered major — either in terms of providing
basic or initial ethnographic coverage of particular peoples or on the grounds they offer exceptionally good
reading and present a "feel" for the nature and style of

native life. (Articles are noted only when monographs are lacking for a major group.) The materials considered in this section are restricted to the writings of anthropologists and other professional scholars; explorers' and other early observers' accounts are included in the review of historical documents.

The many regional groups of Algonquian speakers inhabiting the Labrador Peninsula are often segregated into three major areal divisions in the literature — Naskapi of the North Atlantic and Ungava Bay drainages, Montagnais of the Saint Lawrence drainage, and James Bay Cree of the Hudson Bay drainage — but there is little cultural demarcation between them. Ethnologists are coming to refer to all groups collectively as Montagnais-Naskapi.

For the portion of the Labrador Peninsula draining into the Saint Lawrence, the Atlantic, and Ungava Bay — embracing the political divisions of Labrador and the eastern half of Quebec — Lucien M. Turner's report on the "Ethnology of the Ungava District" [252] (stressing the Naskapi) was the major early contribution. Perhaps of greater interest to the general reader is Frank G. Speck's *Naskapi* [235]. The title is somewhat of a misnomer, as the book describes peoples more narrowly designated as Montagnais and is essentially confined to presentation of spiritual and magico-religious life. *Cultural Stability and Change among the Montagnais Indians of the Lake Melville Region of Labrador* by John T. McGee [162] offers a general description of this Atlantic drainage group in the mid-twentieth century. Georg Henriksen's *Hunters in the Barrens* [97] is a recent and perceptive analysis of the two ways of life of the Naskapi trading into Davis Inlet on the North Atlantic coast. It emphasizes the activities and social relations of the people summering at the trading post in contrast to the traditional values and modes of interaction mobilized when hunting caribou in the interior. Rolf Knight's short monograph details *Ecological Factors in the Changing Economy and Social Organization Among the Rupert House Cree* [128] on the southeast coast of James Bay. John J. Honigmann's "Indians of Nouveau-Québec" [110] is an excellent encapsulation of all aspects of life, past and present, of the Subarctic Algonquians east of Hudson Bay.

In *Notes on the Eastern Cree and Northern Saulteaux* Alanson Skinner [225] presented an early survey of the traditional culture of the Cree peoples on both sides of Hudson Bay and included the Northern Ojibwas of Ontario. The culture in earlier times of one group of Cree on the west side of James Bay is recreated in Honigmann's paper, "The Attawapiskat Swampy Cree: An Ethnographic Reconstruction" [108]. Leonard Mason's *The Swampy Cree: A Study of Acculturation* [153] charts the course of cultural adaptation and change among Oxford House Cree of Manitoba from the 1600s to 1940. No definitive monograph exists for the western extension (as far as Alberta) of Subarctic Cree — who with the "Swampies" of Northern Ontario and Manitoba may be collectively designated the "Western Woods Cree." Edward S. Curtis, however, has provided a historical and cultural summation under that title [38] and in the "Appendix" to the chapter [39].

The other major division of Algonquian-speaking peoples of the Subarctic, the Ojibwas of boreal Ontario and Manitoba, are but part of the Ojibwa nation: a people extending beyond the Subarctic into the mixed hardwood and conifer forest of northern Michigan, Wisconsin, and Minnesota (where they are also known as Chippewas) and into the northeastern Plains (Plains Ojibwas). Limiting discussion to those Ojibwa peoples within the northern coniferous or boreal forest, three publications (in addition to Skinner's *Notes* [225]) constitute major contributions. The topics in Edward S. Roger's study *The Round Lake Ojibwas* [209] range from the environment to the religious life of this Ontario group. Robert W. Dunning's account of *Social and Economic Change Among the Northern Ojibwa* [50] focuses on the people of the Pekangikum Lake area in northern Ontario, who may be more narrowly classified as Saulteaux. Several papers now classics in psychological anthropology are contained in A. I. Hallowell's selection of his writings, *Culture and Experience* [80]. Hallowell's field research and reflections upon the area around Lake Winnipeg's eastern shore concentrated on that division of Ojibwas known as Saulteaux (from their earlier home in the Sault Sainte Marie region). His essays, of great insight and style, provide a sensitive picture of the spiritual and psychological life of the Saulteaux.

Moving into the western two-thirds of Subarctic North America, the domain of the Athapaskan-speaking peoples, the Métis can appropriately be introduced — for the Subarctic Métis count in their linguistic ancestry Algonquian and Athapaskan as well as European elements. In his sympathetic and readable account of the *Metis of the Mackenzie District*, Richard Slobodin [227] distinguished between the predominantly Red River origins (French–Cree) of the Métis of the upper (or southern) Mackenzie region and the Scotch-English–Athapaskan heritage of the "Northern Métis" of the lower Mackenzie.

Abutting the Western Woods Cree are the Athapaskan Chipewyan of northern Manitoba, Saskatchewan, Alberta, and the Northwest Territories. Considering their numbers (appoximately four to five thousand), great spatial range, and role as the first Athapaskans in the fur trade, it is surprising no definitive ethnography of the Chipewyan exists. The first professional monograph was Kaj Birket-Smith's *Contributions to Chipewyan Ethnology* [17]. Birket-Smith spent only a brief period among the Chipewyan of Fort Churchill and relied heavily upon information from the local priest and upon materials gleaned from earlier non-academic observers. Not monographs, but excellent summaries from scattered sources are: Edward S. Curtis's "The Chipewyan" [38] and its "Appendix" [39] (which contains substantial contributions of his own data), and recently, "The Chippewyan" by William H. Oswalt [190]. VanStone documented contemporary village life in *The Changing Culture of the Snowdrift Chipewyan* [256]. The richest, most engrossing account of Chipewyan life is by the eighteenth-century explorer Samuel Hearne, whose work is detailed below.

North of the Chipewyan in the western Shield were the Yellowknives — given a distinctive cognomen in the early historic literature but culturally and dialectically a division of the Chipewyan nation. In "Yellowknives, Quo Iverunt?" Beryl C. Gillespie [67] reviewed the ethnohistory of the Yellowknives and accounted for their "disappearance" in the twentieth century. From a summer's field work in 1913, J. Alden Mason provided the first professional report on Yellowknife, Slave, and Dogrib Indians in *Notes on the Indians of the Great Slave Lake Area* [152].

Other Athapaskans exploiting the western edge of the Shield and adjacent Mackenzie Lowlands were the Dogrib, the Hare, and the Bearlake Indians (or Satudene). The basic work on the latter is Cornelius Osgood's "The Ethnography of the Great Bear Lake Indians" [182]. "Les Chitra-gottinéké" by the French anthropologist Jean Michéa [169] views the Mountain Indians, a band exploiting the Cordillera to the west but trading into the fur post frequented by the Bearlake Indians. *The Trail of the Hare* is a recent study of that tribe by Joel S. Savishinsky [223]. Although more numerous than the groups just mentioned, the Dogrib lack a basic ethnography. A summary of Dogrib ethnohistory and lifeways is presented in Helm's "The Dogrib Indians" [89]. The two Athapaskan divisions of the southern Mackenzie drainage, the Slave and the Beaver, are each represented by a basic ethnography: Honigmann's *Ethnography and Acculturation of the Fort Nelson Slave* [104] and an earlier report, Pliny Earle Goddard's *The Beaver Indians* [69]. A more particularistic monograph is Helm's *The Lynx Point People: The Dynamics of a Northern Athapaskan Band* [86], an in-depth study of a small community of Slave Indians residing on the banks of the Mackenzie River.

Jenness's *The Sekani Indians of British Columbia* [120] offers the basic ethnography of these Cordilleran people, a historical offshoot of the Beaver. For their neighbors to the north and south, the Kaska and the Carrier, the standard ethnographies are, respectively, Honigmann's two volumes, *The Kaska Indians: An Ethnographic Reconstruction* [107] and *Culture and Ethos of Kaska Society* [106] and Jenness's *The Carrier Indians of the Bulkley River, Their Social and Religious Life* [121]. The essay by Irving Goldman "The Alkatcho Carrier of British Columbia" [71] provides a brief but valuable account of the traditional culture and ethnohistory of that group of Carrier up to about 1940. In 1894, Franz Boas recovered data on the history and culture of "The Tinneh Tribe of Portland Inlet, the Ts'ets'a̅ᶥut" [20], who became extinct as a group in the nineteenth century. No recent general ethnographic accounts of the "Tahltan" or the "Chilcotin" of British Columbia exist (except in *The Subarctic* under those titles as respective chapters by Bruce B. MacLachlan [148] and Robert B. Lane [135]). An ethnography of *The Tahltan Indians* is by George T. Emmons [54]. James A. Teit's "Field Notes on the Tahltan and Kaska Indians, 1912–1915" [244] is an additional source on the traditional cultures of those groups.

The Tutchone of the Yukon Territory are well presented in Catharine McClellan's record of their history and traditions, *My Old People Say* [160]. The Tagish and the Inland Tlingit (Atlin and Teslin bands) are two small groups on the borders of Tutchone territory distinguished in a brief report, "The Inland Tlingit" by McClellan [154] (with additional materials in *My Old People Say*).

The Kutchin people occupy the northern half of the Yukon Territory and extend into both the Northwest Territories and Alaska. There is available a basic ethnography, Osgood's *Contributions to the Ethnography of the Kutchin* [183]. A useful companion, Slobodin's study of *The Band Organization of the Peel River Kutchin* [226] provides an account of the experiences of that eastern Kutchin group within the historic era, as well as a felling for the country and the temper of the people. As an areal complement to Slobodin's monograph, the ethnography of a western division of Kutchin is recorded in Robert A. McKennan's *The Chandalar Kutchin* [164]. In *The Han Indians: A Compilation of Ethnographic and Historical Data on the Alaska–Yukon Boundary Area* Osgood [189] exhaustively pulled together the data from various thin accounts to reconstruct the cultural attributes of the traditional Han. For the peoples of central interior Alaska, by far the fullest study is that of the Ingalik contained in Osgood's three volumes: *Ingalik Material Culture* [186], *Ingalik Social Culture* [187], and *Ingalik Mental Culture* [188]. As in his other ethnographies, Osgood concentrated on the reconstruction of aboriginal culture. Although the peoples of the McGrath area were tentatively designated by Osgood as Ingalik, Edward H. Hosley in "The Kolchan: Delineation of a New Northern Athapaskan Indian Group" [114] has succinctly argued that they should be recognized as a dialectically and socially distinct group.

Osgood's classification of "groups" (he eschewed the term "tribes") in *The Distribution of the Northern Athapaskan Indians* [184] differentiated between the Nabesna of the upper Tanana River and the Tanana Indians proper. Robert McKennan has effectively argued in *The Upper Tanana Indians* [163] that any such distinction is overly precise. This work on the Upper Tanana (formerly "Nabesna") is the only basic ethnography available for the Tanana River Indians.

Although Koyukon people in the central plateau of Alaska received a number of brief references in the earlier literature, no definitive ethnography has been published. A summary ethnographic essay, Annette McFayden Clark's "Koyukon" [30], is forthcoming.

The Tanaina and Ahtna occupy the lands south of the Alaska Range in the relatively temperate North Pacific zone. We are again indebted to Osgood for his reconstruction of traditional culture in *The Ethnography of the Tanaina* [185]. It is to be hoped that the research undertaken by McClellan and Frederica de Laguna on the traditional culture of the Ahtna will see publication, for no basic ethnography is now available. They present a condensed record in "Ahtna," a chapter in *The Subarctic* [161].

Prehistory

For other than the professional archaeologist, archaeological interpretations and syntheses that are not the latest are apt to be misleading. Most of the archaeological evidence on the prehistory of the Subarctic has been accumulated only within the last fifteen years. Therefore pioneer syntheses, such as Richard S. MacNeish's "A Speculative Framework of Northern North American Prehistory as of April 1959" [150], are undergoing continuing modification. The most current syntheses and interpretations of Subarctic prehistory will be published as chapters in *The Subarctic.* They are: J. V. Wright's "The Prehistory of the Shield" [272]; William C. Noble's "Prehistory of the Great Slave Lake and Great Bear Lake Region" [181]; and Donald W. Clark's "Prehistory of Alaska, the Cordillera, and the Mackenzie Valley" [31]. Until these see publication, the seventh and eighth chapters of *An Introduction to North American*

Archaeology, I by Gordon R. Willey [265] provide a recent summary of Subarctic prehistory. In "Toward a Pre-history of the Na-Dene" Don E. Dumond [48] has com-bined linguistic and archaeological evidence in a inter-pretation of the prehistory of the Subarctic Athapaskans since the terminal Pleistocene.

Histories and Historical Materials

The impetus for the French, British, and Russian penetration of Subarctic North America can be ascribed to a single goal — fur. From the Saint Lawrence River region (after 1670) and Hudson Bay (after 1770), traders pushed into the interior Subarctic and across the conti-nent until checked by the difficulties of maintaining footholds in the Cordillera. On the other side of the Continental Divide, the Russians held to the coast and archipelago of Alaska; until the second quarter of the nineteenth century, the Tanaina and Ahtna were the only Alaskan Athapaskans in regular contact with trad-ers. Through the same period, the aggressive tribes of the Northwest Coast blocked traders' penetration of the western watershed of today's northern British Columbia and the Yukon Territory. Thus the interior Alaskan and northern Cordilleran Athapaskans were the last to ex-perience direct or sustained White contact (although trade goods had passed through middleman tribes for several generations). The North American Cordillera, then, represents not only a literal watershed but a historic one; it divides the contact history of the Subarctic Indians into two sectors.

Several summaries of the course and consequences of culture contact between major segments of Subarctic natives and Europeans are available: June Helm and Eleanor B. Leacock, "The Hunting Tribes of Subarctic Canada" [93] (from Labrador to the Mackenzie Lowlands); E. Rogers, "The Fur Trade, the Government, and Central Canadian Indian" [211] (Cree and Ojibwa); Helm, et al., "The Contact History of the Subarctic Athapaskans: An Overview" [92]; and McClellan, "Culture Contacts in the Early Historic Period in Northwestern North America" [157] (as concerns the Yukon Territory and Alaska). For the history of a single people, Joan B. Townsend offered an exemplary combination of archaeological, ethnological, and documentary research in "Tanaina Ethnohistory: An Example of a Method for the Study of Culture Contact" [249] and "The Tanaina of Southwestern Alaska: An Historical Synopsis" [250]. (See also Gillespie [67] on the Yellowknives.)

In the intimacy of their association with native peoples and the richness of their accounts, two early European observers are outstanding. A hundred years after Cartier "discovered" the Saint Lawrence, the Jesuit missionary Paul Le Jeune reported from Quebec to his superiors in France on the progress of his work among the Montagnais. The richest body of his reports constitutes "Document XXIII, Le Jeune's Relation 1634" in *The Jesuit Relations* edited by Reuben Gold Thwaites [247], an account of the winter he traveled with a group of Montagnais inland from the Saint Lawrence River.

Samuel Hearne, Le Jeune's counterpart among the Athapaskans, interlarded his narrative of *A Journey from Prince of Wales's Fort in Hudson's Bay to the Northern Ocean, 1769, 1770, 1771 and 1772* [83, 84] with a detailed account of the Chipewyans with whom he traveled and of their leader Matonabbee. (Prince of Wales's Fort is the present day Fort Churchill.)

Hearne's journeys were under the direction of the Hudson's Bay Company, which by then had been on "the bay" for one hundred years. Company post managers regularly reported back to the home office in London. Two published reports that provide useful information (particularly data on the Cree Indians frequenting the west bayside posts) are James Isham's *Observations on Hudson's Bay 1743* [118] and Andrew Graham's *Observations on Hudson's Bay 1767–91* [75]. These men did not venture from the fort, and some of the material is secondhand. Nonetheless, they provided informative descriptions of Cree life and of the relationship between traders and natives in that era. The Isham publication retains the imaginative spelling of the original document, making it somewhat difficult though engaging to read.

Alexander Mackenzie, an officer of the North West Company (and therefore in competition with the Hudson's Bay Company), provided observations on a number of tribes in his recorded descent of the Mackenzie River to the Arctic Ocean in 1789, and of the Frazer to the Pacific in 1793. In *The Journals and Letters of Sir*

Alexander Mackenzie [147], the sections dealing specifically with Indian cultures are contained within Mackenzie's account of "A General History of the Fur Trade from Canada to the Northwest," wherein he gives "Some Account of the Knisteneaux Indians" (the Cree), followed by "Some Account of the Chipewyan Indians." Writing his *Narrative* in his old age, David Thompson [246], who between the years 1784 and 1807 had worked for both the North West Company and the Hudson's Bay Company as surveyor and explorer, recorded in the chapter on the "Nahathaway Indians" his remembrance of the Western Cree. In a series of "Letters to Mr. Roderic McKenzie between 1807 and 1817" George Keith [124], a North West Company trader, described the beliefs and practices of the Athapaskan Indians of the Liard, Mackenzie, Lac la Martre, and Great Bear Lake regions.

The "Journal—1808 to 1851" kept by Robert Campbell [24], a Chief Factor of the Hudson's Bay Company, contains his account of the initiation of White contact in north central British Columbia; of "a remarkable woman, the Chieftainness of the Nahanies [Tahltan]"; and of the dangerous competition for the Cordilleran Athapaskan trade that pitted the Canadian traders against the "Coast Indians." Clifford Wilson's *Campbell of the Yukon* [267] contains a substantial amount of the "Journal" and places Campbell's narrative in a broader historical context. A view of Campbell through native eyes (and Indian oral history of other early White contacts) is presented by McClellan in "Indian Stories about the First Whites in Northwestern America" [159]. Like Campbell's "Journal," Alexander H. Murray's *Journal of the Yukon 1847–48* [117] provides a valuable first-contact description of another Cordilleran Athapaskan people, the Western Kutchin.

Two important Russian sources on Alaska are now available in translation. Ferdinand Petrovich von Wrangell, General Manager of the Russian-American Company, described "The Inhabitants of the Northwest Coast of America" [260] of the 1830s including Ahtna, Tanaina, and Ingalik. VanStone provided a short, useful "Introduction" to Wrangell's observations [257]. *Lieutenant Zagoskin's Travels in Russian America, 1842–1844* edited by Henry N. Michael [168] is a major early eye-witness description of the Athapaskan peoples along the Yukon and Kuskokwim rivers of Alaska.

For fuller comprehension, the records of native life just cited and those of the next one hundred years must be placed in the historical context of White aims and activities in the Subarctic. After World War II, the complex purposes of national governments and multinational corporations began increasingly to structure the native experience. But before the recent era—and except for the White man's gold craze that intermittently broke barriers of people and terrain from northern British Columbia to interior Alaska between the 1850s and 1900—White residents of the Subarctic had one of two goals: as a trader, the promotion of the fur trade; or as a missionary, the proselytization of the Indian. In either case, the Indian was the central element. Harold A. Innis has written the outstanding study of *The Fur Trade in Canada* [117]. His book is invaluable to the understanding of the course of White trade expansion and competition, economic fluctuation, and technological change and the effects on Indian life from 1500 to the third decade of the twentieth century. Alfred G. Bailey has assembled the documentary evidence on *The Conflict of European and Eastern Algonkian Cultures 1504–1700* [9] in all spheres — economic, social, moral, and ideational. Arthur J. Ray's study of *Indians in the Fur Trade* [203] deals only with the peoples on and beyond the southern periphery of the central Subarctic. However, his re-creation of various Indian groups' role "as hunters, trappers and middlemen" in the fur trade aids in understanding the broader Subarctic picture. In "The Indian Traders" Edwin E. Rich [205] explored Indian perceptions, attitudes, and styles of trade — so at variance with the outlook of the French and English with whom they dealt. Adrien G. Morice's *History of the Northern Interior of British Columbia* [173] is a readable account of the Indians, traders, and missionaries in that area to the beginning of the twentieth century.

"Some Ethnological Aspects of the Russian Fur Trade" by Natalie B. Stoddard [239] reviews that trade in the Pacific watershed from Bering's and Chirikov's landfalls in 1741 until the Alaska Purchase of 1867. The relationships between the Russian-American Company (chartered in 1799) and the Aleut and Tlingit peoples, those between Tlingit traders and the Athapaskans of the interior, and the nature of the American and British "ship trade" which "cut into the profits of the Russian-American Company and affected Russian relationships with the native peoples" are briefly but clearly summarized. Vladimir Gsovski chronicled the *Russian Administration of Alaska and the Status of the Alaskan Natives* [76]. (Valuable appendixes include Russian accounts of native tribes and listings of Russian source materials available in the Library of Congress.) In *The Native Races of the Pacific States,* the nineteenth-century historian Hubert Howe Bancroft [10] classified the Pacific drainage Athapaskans and summarized the ethnological knowledge of the time.* The several "general" histories of Alaska published in recent decades generally ignore the existence of the Alaskan natives — except in those instances when they caused "trouble." Clarence C. Hulley's *Alaska: Past and Present* [115] is a welcome exception.

Marcel Giraud's massive historical study *Le Métis Canadien* [68] is the definitive work on the origins and development of the Red River Métis as a distinctive people and, for a period, as a political force. Briefly, he followed the history of those who moved west and north with the fur trade.

A scholarly and balanced history of the relations of various Christian missionary organizations with the

*Other works of Bancroft containing material relevant to Subarctic Indian history are *History of Alaska* [12], *History of British Columbia* [13], and *History of the Northwest Coast* [11].

Indians of the Subarctic is needed. Clerics have written
the major histories of missionary activity in the Subarctic,
and these suffer from a surfeit of sectarian self-praise
and a dearth of information about the Indian converts.
Three missionary histories for the Canadian scene are:
Morice, *History of the Catholic Church in Western Canada*
[174]; Pierre Duchaussois, *Mid Snow and Ice* [47], an
account of the Oblate order in the Lake
Athabasca–Mackenzie River region (which contains useful historical data in the appendix); and T. C. B. Boon,
The Anglican Church from the Bay to the Rockies [21]. In
"L'Honorable Compagnie de la Baie-d'Hudson et les
missions dans l'Ouest canadien," Gaston Carrière, O. M. I.
[26] documented relationships and attitudes of missionaries and Hudson Bay Company officials *vis-à-vis* one
another's aims and activities. Frank A. Peake addressed
the same topic more briefly in "Fur Traders and
Missionaries" [193]. In exerpting "Journals of Nineteenth Century Russian Priests to the Tanaina: Cook
Inlet, Alaska," Townsend [251] provided a summary of
Russian Orthodox missionary activity in southwestern
Alaska and included helpful comments on the text. A
surviving fragment of " 'A Daily Journal Kept by the
Rev. Father Juvenal, One of the Earliest Missionaries to
Alaska, 1796– ' " edited by Bernard G. Hoffman [102]
records the deteriorating relations between that Russian
missionary and a group of Tanaina, culminating in his
death at their hands in 1796.

Not until the results of field work by certain professional anthropologists became available did records of the life of Subarctic peoples begin to achieve the richness offered by the early observers Le Jeune and Hearne. In the last half of the nineteenth century a few new ethnological reports were published. Three Hudson's Bay Company officers provided descriptions for the records of the Smithsonian Institution: "The Eastern Tinneh" by Bernard R. Ross [220] deals with cultural characteristics of the Athapaskans of the Mackenzie drainage; an account of the Eastern Kutchin or "Loucheux Indians" by William L. Hardisty [81]; and a report on "The Kutchin Tribes" in general by Strachan Jones [122]. *Alaska and Its Resources,* an 1870 publication by Willian H. Dall [40] deals with the history and resources of the then recently acquired territory. However, some of Dall's cultural–linguistic classifications of Alaska's Athapaskan groups have since been refuted. Ivan Petroff surveyed the demography, ethnography, and history of native peoples in "The Population and Resources of Alaska, 1880" [199]. Other records in the same United States Senate Report, *Compilation of Narratives of Explorations in Alaska* [199], include brief and usually superficial observations on Indian groups. In his "Report on an [1887] Exploration in the Yukon District, N.W.T., and Adjacent Portion of British Columbia" George M. Dawson [42] described the region and earlier explorations and in Appendix II provided "Notes on the Indian Tribes."

Sir John Richardson, participating in the search for the lost ships of Sir John Franklin, included in his *Arctic Searching Expedition* [206] the chapters "On the Kutchin or Loucheux" (with much of the material taken from Murray's then unpublished "Journal") and "Of the 'Tinnè or Chepewyans" (in which he included some of his own observations of Dogrib and Hare Indians that frequented the Great Bear Lake area). Based both on experiences in Franklin search expeditions and ten years' residence as surgeon at Moose Factory, John Rae wrote "On the Condition and Characteristics of Some of the Native Tribes of the Hudson's Bay Company's Territories" [202]. He remarked favorably upon the Catholic clerics' influence on the Indian and commented, "As a rule, it is thought that the officials of the Hudson's Bay Company have performed their duties to the Indians fairly well." This favorable judgment is in marked contrast to the opinion of John McLean, whose *Notes of a Twenty-Five Years' Service in the Hudson's Bay Territory* [166] (ranging from Hudson Bay to the Cordillera) mounts a sustained attack on the policies of "The Honorable Company" and their effects on Indian well-being.

In the mid-nineteenth century, the Roman Catholic Oblates of Mary Immaculate began vigorous proselytization in Subarctic Canada. Two missionaries of that order, Fathers Petitot and Morice, were astonishingly prolific writers. (Fortunately, their extensive publications have recently received the attention of bibliographers: Donat Savoie,"Bibliographie d'Emile Petitot, Missionaire dans le Nord-Ouest Canadien" [224] and Carrière, "Adrien-Gabriel Morice, O.M.I. (1859–1938) Essaie de bibliographie" [27].) Emile Petitot made several classifications of the Athapaskan speaking peoples, one being contained in his *Monographie des Dènès-Dindjié* [196]. His two most vivid works are narratives of travel and missionary activity among Mackenzie drainage Athapaskans, wherein he chronicled day-to-day encounters and events: *Autour du Grand Lac des Esclaves* [197] and *Exploration de la Region du Grand Lac des Ours* [198]. Father Morice was a practicing ethnologist of the period; he knew best the Carrier Indians. Of his scores of ethnological publications, perhaps the best for the general reader is "The Western Dénés — Their Manners and Customs" [172].

From the 1850s on, other White men embarked on travel tours of the Subarctic for reasons of profession or pleasure. In most of their subsequent accounts, the material on Indians is too sparse, superficial, and supercilious to warrant mention. Henry Y. Hind's narrative of his *Explorations in the Interior of the Labrador Peninsula* [99] in 1861 is a pleasant exception. He made no attempt to produce an ethnographic record, but his sketches of the character and activities of the Montagnais and Naskapi whom he met and traveled with are sympathetic and well rounded. Frederick Whymper's account of his *Travel and Adventure in the Territory of Alaska* [264] in the same decade is more shallow but is useful because of the paucity of other contemporary accounts of the interior Indians.

(A more concise version is his "Russian America, or 'Alaska': the Nature of the Youkon River and Adjacent Country" [263].) One of the Klondike gold-rushers, Edwin Tappan Adney authored and illustrated "Moose Hunting with the Tro–chu–tin" [1] (now known as the Han). During the early years of this century, David E. Wheeler spent a year in travel with the Dogribs in the region between Great Slave and Great Bear lakes. His lively narrative "The Dog-Rib Indian and His Home" [262] ends as he joined company with the anthropologist J. Alden Mason to travel the several hundred miles by canoe to "modern" transport in the south. Frank Russell's *Explorations in the Far North* [221] in 1893 and 1894 took him from Iowa City to the Saskatchewan, then to the Mackenzie region, and home by way of Alaska. His account of a Dogrib muskox hunt and the muskox robe trade is one of several perspectives he provided on Subarctic life in that era. From 1910 to 1937 James W. Anderson was a trader at various posts on the shores of Hudson Bay. His *Fur Trader's Story* [3] combines a picture of Cree Indian life with a history of the late classic fur trade.

Indian Accounts and Personal Histories

At the age of sixty-seven, Tom Boulanger wrote *An Indian Remembers* [22], a reminiscence of people and events in his life in northern Manitoba. This trapper's story provides a complement (from an Indian's perspective) to Anderson's *Fur Trader's Story.* In "The Trapper" Maxwell Paupanekis [192], a Cree from Norway House, told some of the tricks of the trade for successful tours on the trap-line. Far to the northwest on the Mackenzie River, the Slave Indian John Tetso recorded his thoughts, experiences, and knowledge of life in "the bush" in exceptionally evocative style. His essays have been published posthumously (he died of pneumonia while in the bush) as *Trapping is My Life* [245]. In *Geniesh: An Indian Girlhood* Jane Willis [266] richly recreated her childhood in Fort George on Hudson Bay and her high school experiences in Sault Sainte Marie. Her "inmate's" view of church residential schools reads well in conjunction with *The School at Mopass* [125] discussed below. Brief but informative and charming accounts of Indian life and culture in the Alaskan interior of the nineteenth century are offered in *According to Momma,* as told by Laura David Anderson [4] and *According to Papa,* as told by David Paul [191].

Here are the News is a compilation of reports by Edith Josie [123], *Whitehorse Star* news correspondent from the Kutchin village of Old Crow, north of the Arctic Circle. The reports of Dora Gully "From Fort Franklin" [77] to the Yellowknife newspaper *News of the North* are equally informative and flavorful. Unfortunately, her excellent chronicles of the pleasures and concerns of life in an Athapaskan community are not available in book form.

Contemporary Conditions

Of the substantial body of publications that regard the recent scene — from the 1950s to the present — and emergent change in Subarctic Indian life, many, perhaps most, are phrased in terms of "problems." Particular reports may stress variously: the submerged economic position of the Subarctic native; "social problems" such as alcohol abuse; political relations *vis-à-vis* government and attendant frustrations; inter-ethnic relations and status differentials between Indian, White, and various ethnic groups; or more broadly, "urbanization" and "modernization." However, these dimensions are apt to be assessed in any analysis of contemporary life. To segregate the materials under particular topics is, therefore, somewhat artificial.

Edward S. Rogers and Father John Trudeau reviewed the nature and impact of urbanizing trends arising from pressures of the Canadian national society on "The Indians of the Central Subarctic of Canada" [218]. William W. Koolage, Jr. in "Conceptual Negativism in Chipewyan Ethnology" [129] examined and rejected the tendency of most investigators to appraise the changing lifeways of the Chipewyan by applying the concepts of "deculturation," "disorganization," and "disintegration." Koolage's charge of "conceptual negativism" could be extended to other analyses of modern Indian life.

Multi-component research reports or research series which treat contemporary socio-economic conditions among substantial sectors of Subarctic natives include:

Profile of the Native People of Alaska by Robert M. Pennington and H. P. Gazeway [194]; *The Indians and Metis of Northern Saskatchewan: A Report of Economic and Social Development* by Helen Buckley, J. E. M. Kew, and J. B. Hawley [23]; *The People of Indian Ancestry in Manitoba: A Social and Economic Study* in three volumes under the direction of Jean H. Lagassé [134]; *Conflict and Culture: Problems of Developmental Change Among the Cree* (of Quebec) edited by Norman A. Chance [29]; and the reports issued by the Mackenzie Delta Research Project. Among the latter are: *Inuvik Community Structure —Summer 1965* by José Mailhot [151]; *The Mackenzie Delta — Domestic Economy of the Native Peoples* by Derek G. Smith [231]; and *New Northern Townsmen in Inuvik* by A. M. Ervin [55]. *The Indians of British Columbia: A Study of Contemporary Social Adjustment* by H. B. Hawthorn, Cyril S. Belshaw, and Stuart M. Jamieson [82] is comprehensive, but the specifics of the situation of the Subarctic Athapaskans of the British Columbia interior often cannot be distinguished from those of the larger coastal and southern Indian populations.

Investigations of socio-economic stratification and inter-ethnic relations between White, Indian, Métis, and/or Inuit include: Honigmann's *Social Networks in Great Whale River* [109]; John and Irma Honigmann's *Arctic Townsmen* [113]; Jacob Fried's "White Dominated Settlements in the Canadian Northwest Territories" [63] and "Urbanization and Ecology in the Canadian Northwest Territories" [64]; and Dunning's "Ethnic Relations and the Marginal Man in Canada"[49].

Clearly an aspect of the broader issue of inter-ethnic relations is the problem of the Indian child's achievement and commitment in the White-oriented (and directed) school system. Honigmann investigated some of the dimensions in *Arctic Townsmen* and specifically in "Integration of Canadian Eskimo, Indians, and Other Persons of Native Ancestry in Modern Economic and Public Life: Evidence from Inuvik" [111]. In *Alaska's Urban Boarding Home Program* Judith Kleinfeld [126] examined interpersonal relationships between native (Eskimo, Aleut, and Indian) secondary students and their boarding home parents. An intensive study of a residential school for Indian children in the Yukon Territory, focusing on how and why educational aims fail, is *The School at Mopass* by A. Richard King [125].

Although some Indian land claims have recently been settled in parts of the Subarctic, notably in the James Bay drainage of Quebec and in Alaska, others (such as those in the Yukon Territory and the Northwest Territories) are in mediation or litigation. Concurrently, federal and sub-federal government relationships and legal responsibilities to persons of "Indian status" are being challenged or redefined. As a result, any review of the present state of Indian rights and land claims is apt to become quickly dated. In "Directed Change and Northern Peoples" Norman Chance [28] summarized the history of United States federal Indian policy as it has affected the Alaskan natives. A similar assessment, "Goodbye, Great White Father-Figure" by George W. Rogers

[219] concludes with a summary history of Alaskan native political development *vis-à-vis* government. Margaret Lantis has reviewed "The Administration of Northern Peoples: Canada and Alaska" [136] and has charted the formation and development of the Alaska Federation of Natives in "The Current Nativistic Movement in Alaska" [137]. In the even more recent publication "Areas of Initiation in the Political Geography of Aboriginal Minorities," Stewart Raby [201] summarized the provisions of the Alaska Native Claims Settlement and placed in international perspective the land claims and native rights movements of the indigenous Subarctic peoples of Alaska and Canada. Douglas Esmond Sanders enumerated the large-scale development projects (hydro-electric dams, gas and oil pipelines) which threaten northern Canadian native lifeways and land rights and assessed government policy in *Native People in Areas of Internal National Expansion: Indians and Inuit in Canada* [222]. *Native Rights in Canada* edited by Peter A. Cumming and Neil H. Mickenberg [37] covers all aspects of native land rights and speaks to some current issues.

Mary Clay Berry's *The Alaska Pipeline: The Politics of Oil and Native Land Claims* [16] is an invaluable documentation of the political complexities and shifting alliances between various interest groups — environmentalist, native, industrial, and governmental — around the issue of the Alaska pipeline from 1969 to the fall of 1974. *As Long As This Land Shall Last* by René Fumoleau, O.M.I. [66] is a richly documented history of Indian life in the

Northwest Territories between 1870 and 1939. This work contains a detailed picture of the confused and questionable circumstances leading to the signing of land cession treaties in 1899 and 1921. At this writing, the Indians of the Northwest Territories are carrying the struggle against the alienation of their land to the courts of Canada — the Fumoleau study is imperative reading for an understanding of the forces that animate these issues.

At the smallest scale of the spectrum of native political relations with national governments, Richard J. Preston considered "Functional Politics in a Northern Indian Community" [200]. For the same Indian group, the Rupert House Cree, Harriet Kupferer's "Impotency and Power" [133] is a case study of the untenable position in which a band chief finds himself — a situation widely duplicated throughout the Subarctic.

Native Newsletters and Newspapers

The newsletters and newspapers of regional and national native organizations offer a way to keep abreast of current events and issues of concern to Subarctic Indians and other native peoples. One of the most prominent is the weekly *Tundra Times,* published by the Eskimo, Indian, Aleut Publishing Company [56]. (Lantis reviewed the history of the *Times* in "The Current Nativistic Movement in Alaska" [137].) Another Alaskan publication is *River Times,* published by the Fairbanks Native Association [57]. *The Native Press,* now published by the

Native Communications Society of the Western Northwest Territories [116], provides bi-monthly settlement news from local Indian correspondents and covers regional problems and issues. *Akwesasne Notes*, published five times yearly by the Mohawk Nation at Roosevelttown, New York [171], largely features reprints of news items and feature stories from Canadian and United States newspapers on topical issues throughout the Americas, but carries substantial material relevant to Subarctic Indians. The *Bulletin* of the Canadian Association in Support of the Native Peoples [25] (an organization of combined White and native membership) covers activities of the Association and major Canadian issues. It publishes feature reports on critical political, economic, and environmental concerns, such as the James Bay Hydroelectric Project.

Traditional Indian Culture and Society

Most major monographs on Subarctic Indians, especially those written before the 1950s, provide more or less extensive inventories of traditional material culture and include information on techniques of manufacture and resource utilization. The ethnographies by Osgood on Alaskan Athapaskans [183, 185, 186, 189] are noteworthy in this respect.

Three cross-tribal compilations on traditional technical culture are outstanding. *The Athapaskans: Strangers of the North* (which carries no author or editor designation) is a photographic presentation of the traveling artifact exhibit prepared by Canada's National Museum of Man [179]. John M. Cooper surveyed the types and distribution of *Snares, Deadfalls and Other Traps of the Northern Algonquians and Northern Athapaskans* [36]. The final chapters of Edwin Tappan Adney and Howard I. Chappelle's *The Bark Canoes and Skin Boats of North America* [2] offer a coherent compilation of the data on the watercrafts of the Subarctic peoples.

Some studies of single groups stress the artifacts of traditional technology, others attend more fully to activities and knowledge (such as techniques of hide preparation, methods of stalking game, knowledge of behavior of fur bearers, and so forth). Excellent reports are available on the Mistassini Cree. In *The Material Culture of the Mistassini* E. Rogers [213] inventoried tools, implements, and devices. His *The Quest for Food and Furs: The Mistassini Cree, 1953–54* [216] emphasizes techniques of environmental utilization, detailing the seasonal subsistence activities of a hunting group of thirteen individuals during a one year period. Julius E. Lips discussed the manufacture and use of artifacts as well as the social organization of Mistassini activities in "Notes on Montagnais-Naskapi Economy." [144]

Reports on aspects of the traditional economy of Athapaskan peoples include: Müller-Wille, "Caribou Never Die!" [175] dealing with Chipewyan hunting in the Fond du Lac area; Helm and Lurie, *The Subsistence Economy of the Dogrib Indians of Lac la Martre* [94] (for whom fish is a major staple); and VanStone, "Changing Patterns of Indian Trapping in the Canadian Subarctic" [255] emphasizing the Chipewyan of the Snowdrift area. An intensive study of all aspects of man–land relationships provided the basis for Richard K. Nelson's recent work on the Chalkyitsik Kutchin, *Hunters of the Northern Forest* [180]. Robert J. Sullivan recorded the annual subsistence round of the Koyukon in *The T'ena Food Quest* [241]. Sullivan discerned how magico-religious beliefs and practices regarding animals are woven into hunting–fishing–trapping practices.

Also concerned with the material basis of existence, some studies selectively stress those features of environment and resource utilization that shape patterns of economic allocation, human groupings, leadership, and other dimensions of social and territorial organization. Such works may also take into account changes in environment through time (and/or across space) and in historic circumstance and opportunity. As a result, many could be described equally as studies in ecology, social organization, or socio-economic ethnohistory. Such an inquiry is Anthony D. Fisher's "The Cree of Canada: Some Ecological and Evolutionary Considerations" [59] which examines the interplay of sets of social, ecological, and historical variables to account for variations in kinds of Cree communities. Most of the Cree were out of the range of the migratory barrenground caribou herds. For a people who lived "like the wolf " on the caribou, James G. E. Smith saw "The Ecological Basis of Chipewyan Socio-Territorial Organization" [232] to lie in their relationship to the taiga–tundra environment and particularly to the habits of the barrenground caribou. In *The Distribution of the Northern Athapaskan Indians*, Osgood [184] briefly indicated that the relatively sedentary life of groups of Pacific drainage Athapaskans was a function of salmon availability. Julian H. Steward also sounded this theme in "Variation in Ecological Adaptation: The Carrier Indians" [238] when he argued that the cultural ecology of the Western Athapaskans (based on salmon surpluses as "anchor points") allowed them enough latitude to adopt aspects of Northwest Coast social patterns.

A number of decades ago, an area of controversy with broad theoretical implications arose in regard to the material basis of existence. The issue was land tenure among the Subarctic Algonquians. Frank G. Speck, a pioneer in Northern Algonquian studies, described and mapped in several publications the "family hunting territories" of eastern Subarctic Algonquians. He concluded that this system of land-holding by family groups was aboriginal — an appraisal that ran counter to established nineteenth-century and Marxist evolutionary formulations of "primitive communism." One of Speck's last papers (co-authored by Loren C. Eiseley) which expounds the argument is "Montagnais-Naskapi Bands and Family Hunting Districts of the Central and Southeastern Labrador Peninsula" [237]. In recent years, several ethnologists have challenged the aboriginality of the family-held territory. They have argued that it is in fact not a hunting but a trapping territory, and was an adaptive response of eastern Algonquian peoples to environmental and economic changes resulting from the fur trade: Eleanor Leacock, *The Montagnais "Hunting Territory" and the Fur Trade* [141]; E. Rogers, *The Hunting Group–Hunting Territory Complex among the Mistassini Indians* [210]; Rolf Knight, "A Re-examination of Hunting, Trapping, and Territoriality Among the Northeastern Algonkian Indians" [127]; and Charles Aldrich Bishop, "The Emergence of Hunting Territories among the Northern Ojibwa" [18]. In setting forth their evidence for post-contact development of the family-held trapping territory system, these authors have constructed economic ethnohistories of those peoples.

In his monograph on the Mistassini, Rogers [210] documented the enduring viability of the small hunting group (usually composed of from three to five closely kin-linked families) as a basic unit of Subarctic Algonquian social structure, albeit the family-trapping-territory-as-property was a post-contact development. Speck had, in fact, proposed "The Family Hunting Band as a Basis of Algonkian Social Organization" [234] in 1915 — a theme taken up recently in "The Cree of Canada" by Fisher [59]. Among recent analysts, Harold Hickerson has challenged the aboriginal importance of the small hunting group in "Some Implications of the Particularity, or 'Atomism,' of Northern Algonkians" [98].

A number of ethnologists dealing with different peoples have come to recognize a basic comparability in socio-territorial organization from Quebec to central Alaska. They set forth "levels" of socio-territorial groupings and their characteristics (size, kin-composition, nucleation *versus* dispersal); and explore determinants (ecological and contact–historical) which seem to account for basic congruence, plus variation through space and modification through time. Such studies include: Helm's "Bilaterality in the Socio-Territorial Organization of the Arctic Drainage Dene" [87] and "The Nature of Dogrib Socio-Territorial Groups" [88]; and three papers from the 1965 Ottawa Conference on Band Organization "The Montagnais-Naskapi Band" by Leacock [142], "Band Organization Among the Indians of Eastern Subarctic Canada" by E. Rogers [214], and "Athapaskan Groupings and Social Organization in Central Alaska" by McKennan [165].

People in community with one another must solve the problems of maintaining the social order and of decision making, social control, and leadership. A pioneering inquiry into the nature of social control in a Subarctic hunting society, Julius E. Lips's *Naskapi Law* [143] views the Lake Saint John and Lake Mistassini bands. The traditional leadership role in Subarctic society has generally lacked coercive power or formal investiture or other trappings which give immediately visible "form" to leadership. Comprehension of leadership patterns, therefore, requires rather subtle analysis. Edward Rogers has provided one such study (nothing changes through historic time and circumstance) in "Leadership Among the Indians of Eastern Subarctic Canada" [212]. June Helm MacNeish surveyed the historical literature on the Arctic drainage Athapaskans to reconstruct past forms of leadership in "Leadership Among the Northeastern Athabascans" [149]. Slobodin provided an account and analysis of "Leadership and Participation in a Kutchin Trapping Party" [228] with which he traveled in February and March of 1947.

From Labrador to the Cordillera, the peoples of the Subarctic have organized their kinship relations in terms of ego-based, bilateral reckoning (without corporate kin entities such as unilineal descent groups). The exception was the Saulteaux, who shared with their Southern Ojibwa congeners the principle of totemic affiliation in the male line. Dunning's *Social and Economic Change* [50] examines the patri–clan organization of the Pekangikum group.

Most of the Pacific drainage Athapaskan societies are divided into matrilineal clans and/or phratry–moieties. The Ingalik, Lower Koyukon, Chilcotin, Alkatcho Carrier, and Sekani are the major exceptions. Ethnologists have long been divided as to whether the matrilineal descent groups found among Pacific drainage Athapaskans represent an ancient matrilineal principle (from which other Athapaskan peoples have fallen away) or an adaptive borrowing in consequence of the trading relationships, partnerships, and intermarriages — especially important during the nineteenth century — with those Northwest Coast tribes organized in matrilineal descent groups. Ethnologists working with Pacific drainage Athapaskans have in their writings made an effort to describe the structure of matrilineal or non-unilineal descent groups and their significance in the social system, but comparative studies are few. A generation ago, Goldman included a cross-cultural survey in his effort to comprehend more fully the non-unilineal "crest groups" of the Alkatcho Carrier in their inter-cultural and historical setting, "The Alkatcho Carrier: Historical Background of Crest Prerogatives" [72]. A recent, more intensively comparative study is de Laguna's "Matrilineal Kin Groups in Northwestern North America" [44].

Where unilineal descent groups obtained in the Subarctic, there appears to have been a frequent corollary of cross-cousin marriage (a practice congruent with exogamic rules of unilineal descent groups). Perhaps more interesting, an Eastern Algonquian Subarctic people — organized in terms of hunting groups and loose band affiliations and lacking unilineal descent — have been determined to have approved the marriage of cross-cousins.* William Duncan Strong in "Cross-cousin Marriage and the Culture of the Northeastern Algonkian" [240] was the first ethnologist to report that bilateral

---

*Earlier anthropological formulations did not clearly distinguish permissible cross-cousin marriage from preferred cross-cousin marriage — a point well made by Nelson H. H. Graburn in "Naskapi Family and Kinship" [73]. For this reason, the term "approved" is used here.

cross-cousin marriage still occurred among the Naskapi with whom he worked in the 1920s. The theoretical significance of this practice was explored by Fred Eggan in "Social Anthropology: Methods and Results" [51], a general perspective on the social organization of North American Indians. In "Kin Categories Versus Kin Groups: A Two-Section System without Sections" Robin Ridington [207] argued that the Athapaskan Beaver, although without unilineal descent groups, follow directives of "moieties of the mind" in cross-relative spouse selection. Examining "Co-Affinal Siblingship as a Structural Feature Among Some Northern North American Peoples," Albert C. Heinrich and Russell Anderson [85] weighed alternative reasons for this feature of kin terminology shared by the matrilineal Upper Tanana and the bilateral Fort Liard Slave.

In two regions of the Subarctic are found elaborated ceremonial events which express the belief system through the medium of organized group activity. In both regions, much of the form and content of the ceremonial complexes reflect historical or genetic relationships with neighboring groups outside the Subarctic zone. The Grand Medicine Lodge of the Saulteaux of the Lake Winnipeg area was the northernmost extension of this widespread ritual complex. Hallowell reviewed its historical and intercultural setting in his study, "The Passing of the Midewiwin in the Lake Winnipeg Area" [78]. On the other side of the continent, the Athapaskans of the Pacific drainage manifest several types of feasting and ritual exchange between kin groups and/or local groups that today are often loosely assigned the label "potlatch." Such ceremonial events are described in the general ethnographies of the area. "The Koyukon Feast for the Dead" is analyzed in terms of inter-cultural environment and intra-Koyukon variations by William J. Loyens [146].

A pervasive feature of the Subarctic peoples' spiritual life is the belief in "power" inherent in the universe (often called "medicine" in colloquial English). Power infuses spiritual beings and, through the aid of spiritual helpers, human beings may gain access to power. An Athapaskan conception of power and the ways in which it is experienced and obtained is presented in David M. Smith's *Inkonze: Magico-Religious Beliefs of Contact–Traditional Chipewyan* [230]. The individual's relationship with a guardian spirit or "medicine animal" is the subject of "Beaver Dreaming and Singing" by Robin Ridington [208]. The person who commands exceptional power for curing and/or divination is recognized as an adept, a shaman. McClellan took a historical and culture-contact perspective in analyzing "Shamanistic Syncretism in the Southern Yukon" [155]. *The Role of Conjuring in Salteaux Society* by Hallowell [79] is a richly contextual study of the so-called shaking tent rite, a shamanistic performance limited to the Algonquian peoples.

An individual may malevolently turn his control of supernatural power against others. The extent of concern with and the elaboration of beliefs around witchcraft or sorcery varies among the Subarctic peoples. Edward Rogers evaluated the Cree's limited concern with witchcraft compared with the much more extensive anxieties found among the Ojibwas in "Natural Environment–Social Organization–Witchcraft: Cree versus Ojibwa — A Test Case" [215]. Honigmann concluded that "Witch-Fear in Post-Contact Kaska Society" [105] is a consequence of new stresses engendered under contact conditions. Hallowell considered the psychological aspects of sorcery among the Saulteaux. in several papers collected in *Culture and Experience* [80]: "Fear and Anxiety as Cultural and Individual Variables in a Primitive Society"; "The Social Function of Anxiety in a Primitive Society"; and "Aggression in Saulteaux Society."

Two general studies of magico-religious systems have treated either end of the Subarctic: de Laguna's essay, "The Atna of the Copper River, Alaska: The World of Men and Animals" [43] and Speck's *Naskapi* [235]. In contradistinction to Speck's view, Cooper concluded that *The Northern Algonquian Supreme Being* [35] is an aboriginal concept. Adding another dimension to knowledge of the spiritual life of Subarctic Indians, Slobodin documented "Kutchin Concepts of Reincarnation" [229].

Many of the ethnographies concerned with traditional culture include collections of myths, legends, and folk tales. Writings which attend specifically to this aspect of religious and expressive life range from Goddard's

Beaver Texts [70] in the native language with interlinear translation, to popularizations such as Charles Clay's *Swampy Cree Legends* [32] and Bill Vaudrin's *Tanaina Tales from Alaska* [259], to McClellan's analyses of the cultural contexts of lore and myth in *The Girl Who Married the Bear* [158] (a popular story among the Southern Yukon Indians) and "Wealth Woman and Frogs Among the Tagish Indians" [156]. Ronald Cohen and VanStone's analysis of "Dependency and Self-Sufficiency in Chipewyan Stories" [33] ventures into the domain of psychological anthropology (a field not segregated for special discussion here due to limitations of space).

The so-called windigo psychosis found among the Algonquians is a culturally-standardized behavioral pathology predicated on mythic concepts. It has received much attention and varied etiological arguments. Two major assessments of the evidence, from distinctive perspectives, are *Windigo Psychosis* by Morton I. Teicher [243] and "Psychological Theories of Windigo 'Psychosis' and a Preliminary Application of the Models Approach" by Raymond D. Fogelson [61].

Much of Athapaskan aesthetic styles and standards can be inferred from the artifact forms and decorative motifs displayed by the photographs in *The Athapaskans: Strangers of the North* [179]. Speck directly addressed visual art in "The Double Curve Motive in Northeast Algonquian Art" [233] and "Montagnais Art in Birch-Bark" [236]. In another expressive domain, Regina Flannery briefly reviewed "Some Aspects of James Bay Recreative

Culture" [60]. Considerations of recreative, stylistic, and social components of culture are combined in Michael I. Asch's "Social Context and the Musical Analysis of Slavey Drum Dance Songs" [8] and in *The Dogrib Hand Game* by Helm and Lurie [95]. Ethnographic research into many areas of expressive behavior has been scanty and incomplete. Honigmann has recently surveyed and synthesized available knowledge on "Expressive Aspects of Subarctic Culture" [112] including power, shamanism, ceremonial, recreation, speech use, humor and sarcasm, and the "social personality."

Language

Two forthcoming summary articles on geographical distributions and relationships of the Subarctic North American native languages are "Historical Linguistics and Dialect Geography: Algonquian Languages" by Evelyn M. Todd [248] and "Historical Linguistics and Dialect Geography: Athapaskan Languages" by Michael E. Krauss [131]. Other major summaries concerned with classification and relationships are Harry Hoijer's "The Athapaskan Languages" [103] which deals with the Apachean and Oregon–California groups as well and Krauss's "Na-Dene" [130] which considers the entire phylum of which the Athapaskan language family is a part. Truman Michelson's "Linguistic Classification of Cree and Montagnais-Naskapi Dialects" published in 1939 [170] remains a basic work. Later workers have recognized that modifications and revisions are needed in the Michelson schema. An analysis placing the Cree (including Montagnais-Naskapi) and Ojibwa languages in their total linguistic family perspective is Leonard Bloomfield's "Algonquian" [19]. David H. Pentland, et al. have recently provided a *Bibliography of Algonquian Linguistics* [195].

Most of the materials just cited make for technical reading. For the non-specialist, an excellent introduction to the present state of research and knowledge of the Cree languages of Canada is H. Christoph Wolfart's "The Current State of Cree Language Studies" [269].

In recent years there have been a number of local efforts to provide instruction in the native language of the area. Reports on such activities can be found in the *Newsletter* of the Conference on American Indian Languages Clearinghouse [34]. This informative publication covers the entire field of American Indian linguistics, but each issue carries items of interest on Subarctic language studies. The greatest advances in published materials for language learning have been for Cree. *Meet Cree: A Practical Guide to the Cree Language* by Christoph Wolfart and Janet F. Carroll [270] introduces the basic features of the Cree language, but it is not a teaching manual. C. Douglas Ellis's *Spoken Cree, West Coast of James Bay, Part I* [52] is an extensive manual (accompanied by tapes in the Swampy Cree dialect) which a student can use to pursue competence in this dialect of Cree. Ellis has also published "A Proposed Standard Roman Orthography for

Cree" [53], an effort to reconcile the phonologies of the various Cree dialects.

Three recently published articles indicate the direction of developing research on the cultural and social context of language use: Regna Darnell, "Correlatives of Cree Narrative Performance" [41]; Wolfart, "Boundary Maintenance in Algonquian: A Linguistic Study of Island Lake, Manitoba" [268]; and Keith Basso, "Ice and Travel among the Fort Norman Slave: Folk Taxonomies and Cultural Rules" [14].

Bibliographies and Series

Volume 2: Arctic and Subarctic of the *Ethnographic Bibliography of North America* by George Peter Murdock and revised by Timothy J. O'Leary [176] provides complete coverage of ethnographic materials published on Subarctic North America. Helm's *Subarctic Athapaskan Bibliography 1973* [90] covers ethnographic materials and provides selected entries on biological anthropology, prehistory, historical developments, linguistics, and environment. Arthur E. Hippler and John R. Wood, *The Subarctic Athabascans: A Selected Annotated Bibliography* [100] stresses in the annotations material on emotional, psychological, and expressive components of Athapaskan life. *Bibliography Native Peoples, James Bay Region* compiled by Harvey A. Feit, M. E. Mackenzie, José Mailhot and Charles A. Martijn [58] cites ethnographic, linguistic, and archaeological materials pertaining to the native peoples of Quebec within the James Bay watershed and adjacent groups to the south. More specialized bibliographies are: *A Bibliography of Circumpolar Prehistory* by P. F. Donahue [45]; *Alaskan Archaeology: A Bibliography* by Karen W. Workman [271]; *A Selected Regional Bibliography for Human Geographical Studies of the Native Populations in Central Alaska* by Don C. Foote and Sheila K. MacBain [62]; *Yukon Bibliography* by James R. Lotz [145]; and *Yukon Bibliography Update 1963–1970* by C. Anne Hemstock and Geraldine A. Cooke [96].*

Journals and serials emphasizing Subarctic ethnology, native history, and prehistory include: *Arctic Anthropology* [6]; *Anthropological Papers of the University of Alaska* [5]; *Western Canadian Journal of Anthropology* [261]; *The Beaver* [15]; *The Musk-Ox* and *Papers of the Musk-Ox Circle* [178]; *Recherches amérindiennes au Québec* [204]; *Arctic Bibliography* [7]; and the *Mercury Series* of Canada's National Museum of Man [167].

*As this essay was going to press, the author was able to assess an additional bibliography. This work emphasizes linguistics, but also contains many useful citations (including location) of unpublished materials in all fields of anthropology: Richard T. Parr. 1974. *A Bibliography of the Athapaskan Languages*. National Museum of Man, Mecury Series, Ethnology Division Paper:14. Ottawa: National Museums of Man.

Recommended Works

For the Beginner

[74]   Nelson H. H. Graburn and B. Stephen Strong, *Circumpolar Peoples.*

[91]   June Helm, ed., *The Subarctic.*

[119]   Diamond Jenness, *The Indians of Canada.*

[242]   John R. Swanton, *The Indian Tribes of North America.*

[253]   U. S. Federal Field Committee, *Alaska Natives and the Land.*

For a Basic Library Collection

[9]   Alfred G. Bailey, *The Conflict of European and Eastern Algonkian Cultures.*

[66]   René Fumoleau, *As Long As This Land Shall Last.*

[74]   Nelson H. H. Graburn and B. Stephen Strong, *Circumpolar Peoples.*

[79]   A. Irving Hallowell, *The Role of Conjuring in Salteaux Society.*

[83]
or [84] Samuel Hearne, *A Journey.*

[91]   June Helm, ed., *The Subarctic.*

[97]   Georg Henriksen, *Hunters in the Barrens.*

[125]   A. Richard King, *The School at Mopass.*

[160]   Catharine McClellan, *My Old People Say.*

[203]   Arthur J. Ray, *Indians in the Fur Trade.*

[227]   Richard Slobodin, *Metis of the Mackenzie District.*
[235]   Frank G. Speck, *Naskapi.*
[253]   U. S. Federal Field Committee, *Alaska Natives and the Land.*
[258]   James W. VanStone, *Athapaskan Adaptations.*
[266]   Jane Willis, *Geniesh: An Indian Girlhood.*

Bibliographical List
*Denotes items suitable for secondary school students.

*[1]   Adney, Edwin Tappan. 1900. "Moose Hunting with the Tro–chu–tin." *Harper's New Monthly Magazine* 100:494–507.

*[2]   Adney, Edwin Tappan and Chapelle, Howard I. 1964. *The Bark Canoes and Skin Boats of North America.* U. S. National Museum Bulletin:230. Washington, D.C.: Smithsonian Institution.

*[3]   Anderson, James Watt. 1961. *Fur Trader's Story.* Toronto: Ryerson Press.

*[4]   Anderson, Laura David (as told to Audrey Loftus). 1956. *According to Mama.* [Mimeograph] Fairbanks, Alaska: St. Matthew's Episcopal Guild.

[5]   *Anthropological Papers of the University of Alaska.* 1952– . College, Alaska.

[6]   *Arctic Anthropology.* 1962– . Madison: University of Wisconsin Press.

[7]   *Arctic Bibliography*. 1953– . Montreal and Washington, D. C.: Arctic Institute of North America.

[8]   Asch, Michael I. 1975. "Social Context and the Musical Analysis of Slavey Drum Dance Songs. *Ethnomusicology* 19:245–57.

*[9]   Bailey, Alfred Goldsworthy. 1969. *The Conflict of European and Eastern Algonkian Cultures 1504–1700; A Study in Canadian Civilization*. 2nd ed. Toronto: University of Toronto Press.

Bancroft, Hubert Howe.

[10]   1883. *The Native Races of the Pacific States*. 5 vols. Vol. 1 *The Wild Tribes*. San Francisco: A. L. Bancroft and Co.

[11]   1884. *History of the Northwest Coast*. 2 vols. San Francisco: A. L. Bancroft and Co.

[12]   1886. *History of Alaska, 1730–1885*. San Francisco: A. L. Bancroft and Co.

[13]   1887. *History of British Columbia, 1792–1887*. San Francisco: The History Co.

[14]   Basso, Keith H. 1972. "Ice and Travel among the Fort Norman Slave: Fork Taxonomies and Cultural Rules." *Language in Society* 1:31–49.

[15]   *The Beaver*. 1920 — . Winnipeg, Manitoba: The Hudson's Bay Company.

*[16]   Berry, Mary Clay. 1975. *The Alaska Pipeline: The Politics of Oil and Native Land Claims.* Bloomington: Indiana University Press.

[17]   Birket-Smith, Kaj. 1930. *Contributions to Chipewyan Ethnology.* Report of the Fifth Thule Expedition, 1921-24, the Danish Expedition to Arctic North America ... Vol. 6, no. 3. Copenhagen: Gyldendal.

[18]   Bishop, Charles Aldrich. 1970. "The Emergence of Hunting Territories among the Northern Ojibwa." *Ethnology* 9:1–15.

[19]   Bloomfield, Leonard. 1946. "Algonquian." In *Linguistic Structures in Native North America,* ed. Harry Hoijer, et al., pp. 85–129. New York: Viking Fund Publications in Anthropology.

[20]   Boas, Franz. 1895. "The Tinneh Tribe of the Portland Inlet, the Ts' ets' āᶦut." *Report of the Meeting of the British Association for the Advancement of Science* 65:555–69 and 587–92.

[21]   Boon, Thomas Charles Boacher. 1962. *The Anglican Church from the Bay to the Rockies; A History of the Ecclesiastical Province of Rupert's Land and its Dioceses from 1820 to 1950.* Toronto: Ryerson Press.

*[22]   Boulanger, Tom. 1971. *An Indian Remembers: My Life as a Trapper in Northern Manitoba.* Winnipeg, Manitoba: Peguis Pub.

[23]   Buckley, Helen; Kew, J. E. M.: and Hawley, John B. 1963. *The Indians and Metis of Northern Saskatchewan: A Report on Economic and Social Development.* Saskatoon: Centre for Community Studies.

*[24]   Campbell, Robert. 1958. "Journal — 1808 to 1851." In *Two Journals of Robert Campbell.* [Mimeograph] Seattle: Shorey Book Store.

[25]   Canadian Association in Support of the Native Peoples. *Bulletin.* 1960– . Ottawa, Ontario [formerly, Indian–Eskimo Association of Canada, *Bulletin*].

Carriére, Gaston.

[26]   1966. "L'Honorable Compagnie de la Baie-d'Hudson et les missions dans l'Ouest canadien." *Revue de l'Université d'Ottawa* 36:15–39 and 232–57.

[27]   1972. "Adrien-Gabriel Morice, o. m. i. (1859–1938) Essai de bibliographie." *Revue de l'Université d'Ottawa* 42:325–41.

[28]   Chance, Norman A. 1970. "Directed Change and Northern Peoples." In *Change in Alaska: People, Petroleum, and Politics,* ed. George W. Rogers, pp. 180–94. College: University of Alaska Press.

[29]   Chance, Norman A., ed. 1968. *Conflict in Cul-*

ture: Problems of Developmental Change Among the Cree. Working Papers of the Cree Developmental Change Project. Ottawa: Canadian Research Centre for Anthropology, St. Paul University.

*[30]   Clark, Annette McFayden. Forthcoming. "Koyukon." In *The Subarctic,* ed. June Helm. See [91].

[31]   Clark, Donald W. Forthcoming. "Prehistory of Alaska, the Cordillera, and the Mackenzie Valley." In *The Subarctic,* ed. June Helm. See [91].

*[32]   Clay, Charles. 1938. *Swampy Cree Legends; Being Twenty Folk Tales from the Annals of a Primitive, Mysterious, Fast-Disappearing Canadian Race, as told to Charles Clay . . . by Kuskapatchees, the Smokey One.* Toronto: The MacMillan Co. of Canada.

[33]   Cohen, Ronald and VanStone, James W. 1964. "Dependency and Self-Sufficiency in Chipewyan Stories." In *Contributions to Anthropology 1961–1962, Part II.* National Museum of Canada, Bulletin:194, pp. 29–55. Ottawa: Department of Northern Affairs and National Resources.

[34]   Conference of American Indian Languages Clearinghouse. *Newsletter.* 1972– . Arlington, Va.: Center for Applied Linguistics.

Cooper, John Montgomery.

*[35]   1934. *The Northern Algonquian Supreme Being.* Catholic University of America Anthropological Series:2. Washington, D.C.: Catholic University of America Press.

[36]   1938. *Snares, Deadfalls and Other Traps of the Northern Algonquians and Northern Athapaskans.* Catholic University of America Anthropological Series:5. Washington, D.C.: Catholic University of America Press.

[37]   Cumming, Peter A. and Mickenberg, Neil H., eds. 1972. *Native Rights in Canada.* 2nd ed. Toronto: The Indian–Eskimo Association of Canada in association with General Pub. Co. Ltd.
Curtis, Edward S.

*[38]   1928. *The Chipewyan. The Western Woods Cree. The Sarsi.* Volume 18 of *The North American Indian, Being a Series of Volumes Picturing and Describing the Indians of the United States and Alaska.* 20 vols., ed. Frederick W. Hodge."The Chipewyan," pp. 3–52; "The Western Woods Cree," pp. 55–87. Cambridge, U.S.A.: The University Press, 1907–30. (Reprinted, New York: Johnson Reprint Corp., 1970.)

[39]   ———. "Appendix: Tribal Summary: The Chipewyan," pp. 147–51 and "The Western Woods Cree," pp. 152–58.

[40]   Dall, William Healey. 1878. *Alaska and its Resources*. London: Samson, Low, Son, and Marston.

[41]   Darnell, Regna. 1974. "Correlates of Cree Narrative Performance." In *Explorations in the Ethnography of Speaking*, eds. Richard Bauman and Joel Sherzer, pp. 315–36. Cambridge: Cambridge University Press.

[42]   Dawson, George Mercer. 1888. "Report on an Exploration in the Yukon District, N.W.T. and Adjacent Northern Portion of British Columbia." In *Annual Report, Geological and Natural History Survey of Canada, Report B 1887–1888*. Montreal: Dawson Bros.

        De Laguna, Frederica.

*[43]   1969/70. "The Atna of the Copper River, Alaska: The World of Men and Animals." *Folk* 11/12:17–26.

[44]   1975. "Matrilineal Kin Groups in Northwestern North America." In *Proceedings: Northern Athapaskan Conference, 1971*, 2 vols., ed. A. McFayden Clark, vol. 1, pp. 17–145. National Museum of Man Mercury Series, Canadian Ethnology Service Paper:27. Ottawa: National Museums of Canada.

[45]   Donahue, P. F. 1973. *A Bibliography of Circumpo-*

lar Prehistory. University of Manitoba Anthropology Papers:2. Winnipeg: Department of Anthropology, University of Manitoba.

[46] Driver, Harold Edson. 1969. *Indians of North America.* 2nd ed., rev. Chicago: University of Chicago Press.

[47] Duchaussois, Pierre. 1937. *Mid Snow and Ice: The Apostles of the North-West.* Ottawa: Missionary Oblates of Mary Immaculate and Ottawa University.

[48] Dumond. Don E. 1969. "Toward a Prehistory of the Na-Dene, with a General Comment of Population Movements among Nomadic Hunters." *American Anthropologist* 71:857–63.

Dunning, Robert William.

[49] 1959. "Ethnic Relations and the Marginal Man in Canada." *Human Organization* 18:117–22.

[50] 1959. *Social and Economic Change Among the Northern Ojibwa.* Toronto: University of Toronto Press.

[51] Eggan, Frederick Russell. 1955. "Social Anthropology: Methods and Results." In *Social Anthropology of North American Indian Tribes,* 2nd ed., ed. Frederick R. Eggan, pp. 485–551. Chicago: University of Chicago Press.

Ellis, Clarence Douglas.

[52]   1962. *Spoken Cree, West Coast of James Bay, Part I.*
Toronto: Anglican Church of Canada.

[53]   1973. "A Proposed Standard Roman Orthography for Cree." *Western Canadian Journal of Anthropology* 3:1–37.

*[54]   Emmons, George Thornton. 1911. *The Tahltan
Indians.* University of Pennsylvania Museum
Anthropological Publications:4. Philadelphia:
University Museum.

[55]   Ervin, A. M. 1968. *New Northern Townsmen in
Inuvik.* Mackenzie Delta Research Project. Ot-
tawa: Northern Co-Ordination and Research
Centre, Department of Indian Affairs and
Northern Development.

[56]   Eskimo, Indian, Aleut Publishing Company.
Tundra Times. 1962– . Fairbanks, Alaska.

[57]   Fairbanks Native Association. *River Times.*
1972–   . Fairbanks, Alaska.

[58]   Feit, Harvey A.; Mackenzie, M. E.; Mailhot,
José; and Martijn, Charles. 1972. *Bibliography
Native Peoples, James Bay Region.* Recherches
amérindiennes au Québec, Bulletin d'Information, vol. 2, spécial 1. Montreal: Société des
recherches améridiennes au Québec.

[59]   Fisher, Anthony D. 1969. "The Cree of Canada: Some Ecological and Evolutionary Considerations." *Western Canadian Journal of Anthropology.* (Special Issue: *Cree Studies*) 1:7–19.

[60]   Flannery, Regina. 1936. "Some Aspects of James Bay Recreative Culture." *Primitive Man* 9:49–56.

[61]   Fogelson, Raymond D. 1965. "Psychological Theories of Windigo 'Psychosis' and a Preliminary Application of a Models Approach." In *Context and Meaning in Cultural Anthropology,* ed. Melford E. Spiro, pp. 74–99. New York: Free Press.

[62]   Foote, Don Charles and MacBain, Sheila K. 1964. *A Selected Regional Bibliography for Human Geographical Studies of the Native Populations of Central Alaska.* Geography Department Publication:12. Montreal: McGill University Press.

Fried, Jacob.

[63]   1963. "White-Dominated Settlements in the Canadian Northwest Territories." *Anthropologica* 5:57–66.

[64]   1964. "Urbanization and Ecology in the Canadian Northwest Territories." *Arctic Anthropology* 2:56–60.

[65]   Fried, Jacob, ed. 1955. *A Survey of the Aboriginal Populations of Quebec and Labrador.* Eastern Canadian Anthropological Series:1. Montreal: McGill University Press.

*[66]   Fumoleau, René. 1975. *As Long As This Land Shall Last.* Toronto: McCleland and Stewart, Ltd.

*[67]   Gillespie, Beryl C. 1970. "Yellowknives: Quo Iverunt?" In *Migration and Anthropology,* Proceedings of the 1970 Annual Spring Meeting of the American Ethnological Society, ed. Robert F. Spencer, pp. 61–71. Seattle: University of Washington Press.

[68]   Giraud, Marcel. 1945. *Le Métis Canadien; son rôle dans l'histoire des provinces de l'Ouest.* Travaux et Memoires de l'Institut d'Ethnologie:44. Paris: Institut d'Ethnologie.

Goddard, Pliny Earle.

[69]   1917. *Beaver Texts.* Anthropological Papers of the American Museum of Natural History:10, pt. 5. New York: The Trustees.

[70]   1917. *Beaver Texts.* Anthropological Papers of the American Museum of Natural History:10, pt. 5. New York: The Trustees.

Goldman, Irving.

[71]   1940. "The Alkatcho Carrier of British Colum-
        bia." In *Acculturation in Seven Indian Tribes*, ed.
        Ralph Linton, pp. 333–89. New York: D.
        Appleton–Century Co.

[72]   1941. "The Alkatcho Carrier: Historical Back-
        ground of Crest Prerogatives." *American An-
        thropologist* 43:396–418.

[73]   Graburn, Nelson H. H. 1975. "Naskapi Family
        and Kinship." *Western Canadian Journal of An-
        thropologist* 43:396–418.

*[74]   Graburn, Nelson H. H. and Strong, Stephen B.
        1973. *Circumpolar Peoples: An Anthropological
        Perspective.* Pacific Palisades, Calif.: Goodyear
        Pub. Co. Inc.

*[75]   Graham, Andrew. 1969. *Andrew Graham's Obser-
        vations on Hudson's Bay, 1767–91*, ed. Glyndwr
        Williams. The Hudson's Bay Record Society:27.
        London: The Hudson's Bay Record Society.

[76]   Gsovski, Vladimir. 1950. *Russian Administration
        of Alaska and the Status of the Alaskan Natives.*
        Senate Document No. 152, 81st Congress, 2nd
        session. Washington, D.C.:U. S. Government
        Printing Office.

[77]   Gully, Dora. "From Fort Franklin." Column

regularly appearing in the weekly newspaper *News of the North,* Yellowknife, N.W.T.

Hallowell, Alfred Irving.

[78]   1936. "The Passing of the Midewiwin in the Lake Winnipeg Region."*American Anthropologist* 38:32–51.

*[79]   1942. *The Role of Conjuring in Salteaux Society.* Publications of the Philadelphia Anthropological Society:2. Philadelphia: University of Pennsylvania Press; and London: Oxford University Press.

[80]   1955. *Culture and Experience.* Philadelphia: University of Pennsylvania Press. (Reprinted; New York: Schocken Books, 1967.)

[81]   Hardisty, William L. 1867. "The Loucheux Indians." In *Annual Report for the Year 1866 of the Smithsonian Institution,* pp. 311–20. Washington, D. C.: U. S. Government Printing Office.

[82]   Hawthorn, H. B.; Belshaw, Cyril S.; and Jamieson, Stuart M. 1958. *The Indians of British Columbia: A Study of Contemporary Social Adjustment.* Berkeley: University of California Press.

Hearne, Samuel.

*[83]   1911. *A Journey from Prince of Wales's Fort in Hudson's Bay to the Northern Ocean in the Years 1769, 1770, 1771, and 1772 . . .* ed. Joseph Burr

Tyrrell. Publications of the Champlain Society:6. Toronto: The Champlain Society.

*[84]   1958. *A Journey from Prince of Wales's Fort in Hudson's Bay to the Northern Ocean in the Years 1769, 1770, 1771 and 1772,* ed. R. Glover. Toronto: Macmillan.

[85]   Heinrich, Albert C. and Anderson, Russell. 1968. "Co-Affinal Siblingship as a Structural Feature Among Some Northern North American Peoples." *Ethnology* 7:290–95.

Helm, June.

[86]   1961. *The Lynx Point People: The Dynamics of a Northern Athaspaskan Band.* National Museum of Canada, Bulletin: 176, Anthropological Series:53. Ottawa: Department of Northern Affairs and National Resources.

[87]   1965. "Bilaterality in the Socio-Territorial Organization of the Arctic Drainage Dene." *Ethnology* 4:361–85.

[88]   1968. "The Nature of Dogrib Socio-Territorial Groups." In *Man the Hunter,* eds. Irven DeVore and Richard B. Lee, pp. 118–25. Chicago: Aldine Press.

*[89]   1972. "The Dogrib Indians." In *Hunters and Gatherers Today,* ed. M. G. Bicchieri, pp. 51–89. New York: Holt, Rinehart and Winston.

[90]   1973. *Subarctic Athapaskan Bibliography 1973*. Iowa City: Department of Anthropology, University of Iowa.

*[91]   Helm, June, ed. Forthcoming. *The Subarctic*. Vol. 6, *Handbook of North American Indians*, gen. ed. William Sturtevant. Washington, D.C.: Smithsonian Institution.

[92]   Helm, June; Alliband, Terry; et al. 1975. "The Contact History of the Subarctic Athapaskans: An Overview." In *Proceedings: Northern Athapaskan Conference, 1971*, ed. A. McFayden Clark, vol. 1, pp. 302–49. See [44].

*[93]   Helm, June and Leacock, Eleanor B. 1971. "The Hunting Tribes of Subarctic Canada." In *North American Indians in Historical Perspective*, eds. Eleanor B. Leacock and Nancy O. Lurie, pp. 343–74. New York: Random House.

Helm, June and Lurie, Nancy Oestriech.

[94]   1961. *The Subsistence Economy of the Dogrib Indians of Lac la Martre in the Mackenzie District of the N. W. T.* Northern Co-ordination and Research Centre, N. C. R. C. 61–3. Ottawa: Department of Indian Affairs and Northern Development.

[95]   1966. *The Dogrib Hand Game*. National Museum of Canada, Bulletin:205, Anthropological

Series:71. Ottawa: Department of the Secretary of State.

[96]   Hemstock, C. Anne and Cook, Geraldine A. 1973. *Yukon Bibliography Update 1963–1970.* Boreal Institute for Northern Studies, Occasional Publication No. 8 (1). Edmonton: University of Alberta.

*[97]   Henriksen, Georg. 1973. *Hunters in the Barrens, the Naskapi on the Edge of the White Man's World.* Newfoundland Social and Economic Studies:12. Newfoundland: Institute of Social and Economic Research, Memorial University of Newfoundland.

[98]   Hickerson, Harold. 1967. "Some Implications of the Theory of the Particularity, or 'Atomism,' of Northern Algonkians." *Current Anthropology* 8:313–43.

[99]   Hind, Henry Youle 1863. *Explorations in the Interior of the Labrador Peninsula, the country of the Montagnais and Nasquapee Indians.* 2 vols. London: Longman, Green, Longman, Roberts, and Green.

[100]   Hippler, Arthur E. and Wood, John R., comps. 1974.*The Subarctic Athabascans, A Selected Annotated Bibliography.* Fairbanks: Institute of Social, Economic and Government Research, University of Alaska.

*[101] Hodge, Frederick Webb, ed. 1907 and 1910. *Handbook of American Indians North of Mexico.* 2 vols. Smithsonian Institution, Bureau of Ethnology. Washington, D.C.: Government Printing Office.

[102] Hoffman, Bernard G., ed. 1952. " 'A Daily Journal Kept by the Rev. Father Juvenal, One of the Earliest Missionaries to Alaska, 1796–' Translated from Manuscript in possession of Rev. Shasnikov in Unalaska." *Kroeber Society Anthropological Papers* 6:26–59.

[103] Hoijer, Harry, et al. 1963. "The Athapaskan Languages." In *Studies in the Athapaskan Languages,* ed. H. Hoijer, pp. 1–29. University of California Publications in Linguistics:29. Berkeley: University of California Press.

Honigmann, John Joseph.

[104] 1946. *Ethnography and Acculturation of the Fort Nelson Slave.* Yale University Publications in Anthropology:33. New Haven: Department of Anthropology, Yale University.

[105] 1947. "Witch-Fear in Post-Contact Kaska Society." *American Anthropologist* 49:222–43.

[106] 1949. *Culture and Ethos of Kaska Society.* Yale University Publications in Anthropology:40. New Haven: Department of Anthropology, Yale University.

[107] 1954. *The Kaska Indians: An Ethnographic Reconstruction.* Yale University Publications in Anthropology:51. New Haven: Department of Anthropology, Yale University.

[108] 1956. "The Attawapiskat Swampy Cree: An Ethnographic Reconstruction." *Anthropological Papers of the University of Alaska* 5:23–82.

[109] 1962. *Social Networks in Great Whale River. Notes on an Eskimo, Montagnais-Naskapi, and Euro-Canadian Community.* National Museum of Canada, Bulletin:178, Anthropological Series:54. Ottawa: Department of Northern Affairs and Natural Resources.

*[110] 1964. "Indians of Noveau-Québec." In *Le Nouveau-Québec; contribution à l'étude de l'occupation humaine,* eds. Jean Malaurie and Jacques Rousseau, pp. 315–73. The Hague: Mouton.

[111] 1973. "Integration of Canadian Eskimo, Indians and Other Persons of Native Ancestry in Modern Economic and Public Life: Evidence from Inuvik." In *Circumpolar Problems: Habitat, Economy and Social Relations in the Arctic,* ed. Gösta Berg, pp. 61–72. Wenner-Gren Center, International Symposium Series:21. Oxford: Pergamon Press.

*[112] Forthcoming. "Expressive Aspects of Subarctic

Culture." In *The Subarctic,* ed. June Helm. See [91].

[113] Honigmann, John Joseph and Honigmann, Irma. 1970. *Arctic Townmen: Ethnic Backgrounds and Modernization.* Ottawa: Canadian Research Centre for Anthropology, St. Paul University.

[114] Hosley, Edward H. 1968. "The Kolchan: Delineation of a New Northern Athapaskan Indian Group." *Arctic* 21:6–11.

*[115] Hulley, Clarence C. 1970. *Alaska: Past and Present.* 3d ed. Portland: Binfords and Mort.

[116] Indian Brotherhood [to April 1975]; Native Communications Society of the Western Northwest Territories. *Native Press.* 1971–.

*[117] Innis, Harold Adams. 1956. *The Fur Trade in Canada, An Introduction to Canadian Economic History.* Rev. ed. Toronto: University of Toronto Press.

*[118] Isham, James. 1949. *James Isham's Observations on Hudson's Bay, 1743 . . .,* ed. Edwin E. Rich. The Hudson's Bay Record Society:12. London: The Hudson Bay Record Society. (Reprinted, Lessingdruckerei in Weisbaden: Kraus Reprint. 1968.)

Jenness, Diamond.

*[119] 1934. *The Indians of Canada.* 2nd ed. National

Museum of Canada, Bulletin:65, Anthropological Series:15. Ottawa: Department of Mines.

[120] 1937. *The Sekani Indians of British Columbia.* Canada Department of Mines and Resources, Bulletin:84, Anthropological Series:20. Ottawa: Department of Mines and Resources.

[121] 1943. *The Carrier Indians of the Bulkley River: Their Social and Religious Life.* Smithsonian Institution, Bureau of Ethnology, Paper: 25, Bulletin: 133, pp. 469–586, Washington, D.C.: U. S. Government Printing Office.

[122] Jones, Strachan. 1867. "The Kutchin Tribes." In *Annual Report for the Year 1866 of the Smithsonian Institution,* pp. 303–27. Washington, D. C.: Government Printing Office.

*[123] Josie, Edith. 1966. *Here Are the News.* Toronto and Vancouver: Clarke, Irwin and Co. Ltd.

[124] Keith, George. 1890. "Letters to Mr. Roderic McKenzie 1807–1817." In *Les Bourgeois de la Compagnie du Nord-Quest; Récits de Voyages, Lettres et Rapports inédits relatifs au Nord-Quest Canadien . . . ,* ed. Louis Francois Rodrique Masson, 2 vols., vol. 2, pp. 261–132. Québec: A. Cote et CIE, 1889–90. (Facsimile reprint, 2 vols., New York: Antiquarian Press, Ltd., 1960.)

*[125] King, Alfred Richard. 1967. *The School at Mopass: A Problem of Identity.* New York: Holt,

Rinehart and Winston. [Mopass is a pseudonymic place name.]

[126]   Kleinfeld, Judith. 1972. *Alaska's Urban Boarding Home Program; Interpersonal Relationships Between Indian and Eskimo Secondary Students and Their Boarding Home Parents.* Institute of Social, Economic, and Government Research. Report: 32. Fairbanks: University of Alaska.

Knight, Rolf.

[127]   1965. "A Re-examination of Hunting, Trapping, and Territoriality among the Northeastern Algonkian Indians." In *Man, Culture and Animals; The Role of Animals in Human Ecological Adjustments*, eds. Anthony Leeds and Andrew P. Vayda, pp. 27–42. Washington, D. C.: American Association for the Advancement of Science.

[128]   1968. *Ecological Factors in the Changing Economy and Social Organization Among the Rupert House Cree.* Anthropology Papers of the National Museum of Canada:15. Ottawa: Department of the Secretary of State.

[129]   Koolage, William W., Jr. 1975. "Conceptual Negativism in Chipewyan Ethnology." *Anthropologica* 17:45–60.

Krauss, Michael E.

[130]   1973. "Na-Dene." In *Current Trends in Linguis-*

tics, vol. 10, ed. Thomas A. Sebeok, pp. 903–78. The Hague: Mouton.

[131] Forthcoming. "Historical Linguistics and Dialect Geography: Athapaskan Languages." In *The Subarctic,* ed. June Helm. See [91].

[132] Kroeber, Alfred Louis. 1939. *Cultural and Natural Areas of Native North America.* Berkeley: University of California Press.

[133] Kupferer, Harriet J. 1966. "Impotency and Power: A Cross-Cultural Comparison of the Effect of Alien Rule." In *Political Anthropology,* eds. Marc. J. Swartz, Victor W. Turner, and Arthur Tuden, pp. 61–71. Chicago: Aldine Pub. Co.

[134] Lagassé, Jean H., director. 1959. *The People of Indian Ancestry in Manitoba: A Social and Economic Study.* 3 vols. Winnipeg: The Department of Agriculture and Immigration.

*[135] Lane, Robert B. Forthcoming. "Chilcotin." In *The Subarctic,* ed. June Helm. See [91].

Lantis, Margaret.

[136] 1966. "The Administration of Northern Peoples: Canada and Alaska." In *The Arctic Frontier,* ed. R. St. J. MacDonald, pp. 89–119. Toronto: University of Toronto Press.

[137] 1973. "The Current Nativistic Movement in

Alaska." In *Circumpolar Problems: Habitat, Economy and Social Relations in the Artic,* ed. Gösta Berg, pp. 99–118. See [111].

Laviolette, Gontran.

[138]   1955. "Notes on the Aborigenes of the Province of Quebec." *Anthropologica* 1:198–211.

[139]   1956. "Notes on the Aborigines of the Prairie Provinces (Manitoba, Saskatchewan, Alberta)." *Anthropologica* 2:107–30.

[140]   1957. "Notes on the Aborigines of the Province of Ontario." *Anthropologica* 3:79–106.

Leacock, Eleanor B.

[141]   1954. *The Montagnais 'Hunting Territory' and the Fur Trade.* American Anthropological Association Memoir:78. Menasha, Wisc.: American Anthropological Association.

[142]   1969. "The Montagnais-Naskapi Band." In *Contributions to Anthropology: Band Societies,* ed. David Damas, pp. 1–17. National Museums of Canada, Bulletin:228, Anthropological Series:84. Ottawa: National Museums of Canada.

Lips, Julius Ernst.

[143]   1947. "Naskapi Law (Lake St. John and Lake Mistassini Bands), Law and Order in a Hunting

Society." *"Transactions of the American Philosophical Society* 37:379–492.

[144] 1947. "Notes on Montagnais-Naskapi Economy." *Ethnos* 12:1–78.

[145] Lotz, James Robert. 1964. *Yukon Bibliography.* Yukon Research Project Series:1. Ottawa: Northern Co-ordination and Research Centre, Department of Northern Affairs and National Resources.

[146] Loyens, William John. 1964. "The Koyukon Feast for the Dead." *Arctic Anthropology* 2:133–48.

*[147] Mackenzie, Sir Alexander. 1970. *The Journals and Letters of Sir Alexander Mackenzie,* ed. W. Kaye Lamb. Cambridge: Cambridge University Press.

*[148] MacLachlan, Bruce B. Forthcoming. "Tahltan." In *The Subarctic,* ed. June Helm. See [91].

[149] MacNeish, June Helm. 1956. "Leadership among the Northeastern Athabascans." *Anthropologica* 2:131–63.

[150] MacNeish, Richard S. 1959. "A Speculative Framework of Northern North American Prehistory as of April 1959." *Anthropologica* 1:7–23.

[151] Mailhot, José. 1968. *Inuvik Community Struc-*

ture – Summer 1965. Mackenzie Delta Research Project:4. Ottawa: Northern Co-ordination and Research Centre, Department of Indian Affairs and Northern Development.

[152]   Mason, John Alden, 1946. *Notes on the Indians of the Great Slave Lake Area.* Yale University Publications in Anthropology:34. New Haven: Department of Anthropology, Yale University.

[153]   Mason, Leonard. 1967. *The Swampy Cree: A Study in Acculturation.* Anthropology Papers of the National Museum of Canada:13. Ottawa: Department of the Secretary of State.

McClellan, Catharine.

[154]   1953. "The Inland Tlingit." *Memoirs of the Society for American Archaeology* 9:47–52.

[155]   1956. "Shamanistic Syncretism in Southern Yukon." *Transactions of the New York Academy of Sciences* (Series 2) 19:130–37.

*[156]   1963. "Wealth Woman and Frogs among the Tagish Indians." *Anthropos* 58:121–28.

[157]   1964. "Culture Contacts in the Early Historic Period in Northwestern North America." *Arctic Anthropology* 2 (2):3–15.

[158]   1970. *The Girl Who Married the Bear.* National Museum of Man, Publications in Ethnology:2. Ottawa: National Museums of Canada.

*[159] 1970. "Indian Stories about the First Whites in Northwestern America." In *Ethnohistory in Southwestern Alaska and the Southern Yukon*, ed. Margaret Lantis, pp. 103–33. Lexington: University of Kentucky Press.

[160] 1976. *My Old People Say: An Ethnographic Survey of Southern Yukon Territory*. National Museum of Man, Publications in Ethnology:6. Ottawa: National Museums of Canada.

*[161] McClellan, Catharine and de Laguna, Frederica. Forthcoming. "Ahtna." In *The Subarctic*, ed. June Helm. See [91].

[162] McGee, John T. 1961. *Cultural Stability and Change Among the Montagnais Indians of the Lake Melville Region of Labrador*. Catholic University of America Anthropological Series:19. Washington, D.C.: Catholic University of America Press.

McKennan, Robert Addison.

[163] 1959. *The Upper Tanana Indians*. Yale University Publications in Anthropology:55 New Haven: Department of Anthropology, Yale University.

[164] 1965. *The Chandalar Kutchin*. Arctic Institute of North America, Technical Paper:17. Montreal: Arctic Institute of North America.

[165] 1969. "Athapaskan Groupings and Social Or-

ganization in Central Alaska." In *Contributions to Anthropology: Band Societies,* ed. David Damas, pp. 93–114. See [142].

*[166] McLean, John. 1932. *Notes of a Twenty-Five Years' Service in the Hudson's Bay Territory,* ed. W. S. Wallace. Champlain Society Publication: 19. Toronto: The Champlain Society. (Facsimile edition, New York: Greenwood Press, 1968.)

[167] *Mercury Series.* 1972– . Ottawa: National Museum of Man, National Museums of Canada.

[168] Michael, Henry N., ed. 1967. *Lieutenant Zagoskin's Travels in Russian America, 1842–44.* Toronto: University of Toronto Press.

[169] Michéa, Jean. 1963. "Les Chittra-gottinéké; essai de monographie d'un groupe Athapascan des montagnes Rocheuses." In *Contributions to Anthropology, 1960,* Part 2, pp. 49–93. National Museum of Canada, Bulletin: 190. Ottawa: Department of Northern Affairs and National Resources.

[170] Michelson, Truman. 1939. "Linguistic Classification of Cree and Montagnais-Naskapi Dialects." Smithsonian Institution, Bureau of American Ethnology, Bulletin 123:67–95.

[171] Mohawk Nation. *Akwesasne Notes.* 1969– . Rooseveltttown, N.Y.

Morice, Adrien Gabriel.

[172] 1890. "The Western Dénés — Their Manners and Customs." *Proceedings of the Canadian Institute 1888-1889* (Series 3) 7:109-74.

*[173] 1904. *The History of the Northern Interior of British Columbia, Formerly New Caledonia.* Toronto: William Briggs.

[174] 1910. *History of the Catholic Church in Western Canada from Lake Superior to the Pacific Ocean (1659–1895).* 2 vols. Toronto: The Mussen Book Co. Ltd.

*[175] Müller-Wille, Ludger. 1974. "Caribou Never Die! Modern Caribou Hunting Economy of the Dene (Chipewyan) of Fond du Lac, Saskatchewan and N. W. T." *Musk-Ox* 14:7-19.

[176] Murdock, George Peter. 1975. *Ethnographic Bibliography of North America.* 4th ed., rev. by Timothy J. O'Leary. 5 vols. Vol. 2, *Arctic and Subarctic.* New Haven: Human Relations Area Files.

*[177] Murray, Alexander Hunter. 1910. *Journal of the Yukon 1847–48,* ed. L. J. Burpee. Publications of the Canadian Archives:4. Ottawa: Government Printing Bureau.

[178] *Musk-Ox.* 1967– . Saskatoon: Institute for Northern Studies, University of Saskatchewan:

Papers of the Musk-Ox Circle are published irregularly at the Institute.

*[179]   National Museum of Man. 1974. *The Athapaskans: Strangers of the North*. Ottawa: National Museums of Canada.

⇒ *[180]   Nelson, Richard K. 1973. *Hunters of the Northern Forest: Designs for Survival among the Alaskan Kutchin*. Chicago: University of Chicago Press.

[181]   Noble, William C. Forthcoming. "Prehistory of the Great Slave Lake and Great Bear Lake Region." In *The Subarctic*, ed. June Helm. See [91].

Osgood, Cornelius.

[182]   1932. "The Ethnography of the Great Bear Lake Indians." In *Annual Report for 1931*, National Museum of Canada, Bulletin:70, pp. 31–97. Ottawa: Department of Mines.

[183]   1936. *Contributions to the Ethnography of the Kutchin*. Yale University Publications in Anthropology:14. New Haven: Department of Anthropology, Yale University.

[184]   1936. *The Distribution of the Northern Athapaskan Indians*. Yale University Publications in Anthropology:7. New Haven: Department of Anthropology, Yale University.

[185]   1937. *The Ethnography of the Tanaina*. Yale Uni-

versity Publications in Anthropology:16. New Haven: Department of Anthropology, Yale University.

[186] 1940. *Ingalik Material Culture*. Yale University Publications in Anthropology:22. New Haven: of Anthropology, Yale University.

[187] 1958. *Ingalik Social Culture*. Yale University Publications in Anthropology:53. New Haven: Department of Anthropology, Yale University.

[188] 1959. *Ingalik Mental Culture*. Yale University Publications in Anthropology:56. New Haven: Department of Anthropology, Yale University.

[189] 1971. *The Han Indians: A Compilation of Ethnographic and Historical Data on the Alaska–Yukon Boundary Area*. Yale University Publications in Anthropology:74. New Haven: Department of Anthropology, Yale University.

*[190] Oswalt, Wendell H. 1973. "The Chippewyan." In *This Land Was Theirs: A Study of the North American Indian*, by Wendell H. Oswalt, 2nd ed. rev., pp. 35–76. New York: John Wiley.

*[191] Paul, David (as told to Audrey Loftus). 1957. *According to Papa*. [Mimeograph] Fairbanks, Alaska: St. Matthew's Episcopal Guild.

*[192] Paupanekis, Maxwell. 1973. "The Trapper." In *People and Pelts; Selected Papers of the Second North*

American Fur Trade Conference, ed. Malvina Bolus, pp. 137–43. Winnipeg: Peguis Pub.

[193]   Peake, Frank A. 1972. "Fur Traders and Missionaries: Some Reflections on the Attitudes of the Hudson's Bay Company Towards Missionary Work Among the Indians." *Western Canadian Journal of Anthropology* (Special Issue: *The Fur Trade in Canada*) 3:72–93.

[194]   Pennington, Robert M. and Gazaway, H. P. 1967. *Profile of the Native People of Alaska (exclusive of the Southeast).* Juneau: U. S. Department of the Interior, Bureau of Indian Affairs.

[195]   Pentland, David H.; Ellis, C. W.; Simpson, C. A.; and Wolfart, H. C. 1974. *A Bibliography of Algonquian Linguistics.* University of Manitoba Anthropology Papers:11. Winnipeg: Department of Anthropology, University of Manitoba.

Petitot, Emile Fortuné Stanislaus Joseph.

[196]   1876. *Monographie des Dènè-Dindjié.* Paris: E. Leroux.

[197]   1891. *Autour du Grand Lac des Esclaves.* Paris: A. Savine.

[198]   1893. *Exploration de la Region du Grand Lac des Ours (Fin des Quinze ans sous le Cercle Polaire).* Paris: Téqui, Libraire-Editeur.

[199]   Petroff, Ivan. 1900. "The Population and Re-

sources of Alaska, 1800." In *Compilation of Narratives of Explorations in Alaska*. Committee on Military Affairs, U. S. Senate Report No. 1023. 56th Congress, 1st session. Washington, D.C.: U. S. Government Printing Office.

[200] Preston, Richard J. 1971. "Functional Politics in a Northern Indian Community." In *Proceedings of the 38th International Congress of Americanists* (1968), 4 vols., vol. 3, pp. 169–78. Stuttgart and Munich: Klaus Renner.

[201] Raby, Stewart. 1975. "Areas of Initiation in the Political Geography of Aboriginal Minorities." *Musk-Ox* 15:39–43.

[202] Rae, John. 1882. "On the Conditions and Characteristics of Some of the Native Tribes of the Hudson's Bay Company Territories." *Journal of the Society of the Arts.* (Part 1) 30: 483–99.

*[203] Ray, Arthur J. 1974. *Indians in the Fur Trade: Their Role as Trappers, Hunters, and Middlemen in the Lands Southwest of Hudson Bay, 1660–1870*. Toronto: University of Toronto Press.

[204] *Recherches amérindiennes au Québec.* 1971– Montreal: Société des recherches amérindiennes au Québec.

[205] Rich, Edwin Ernest. 1970. "The Indian Traders." *The Beaver* (Winter) Outfit 301:4–20.

*[206] Richardson, Sir John. 1851. *Arctic Searching Expedition: A Journal of a Boat-Voyage Through Rupert's Land and the Arctic Sea in search of the discovery ships under the command of Sir John Franklin.* 2 vols. London: Longman, Brown, Green, and Longmans.

Ridington, Robin.

[207] 1969. "Kin Categories Versus Kin Groups: A Two-Section System Without Sections." *Ethnology* 8:460–67.

[208] 1971. "Beaver Dreaming and Singing." *Anthropologica* (Special Issue: *Pilot Not Commander: Essays in Memory of Diamond Jenness,* eds. Pat and James Lotz) 13:115–28.

Rogers, Edward S.

[209] 1962. *The Round Lake Ojibwa.* Occasional Paper 5, Art and Archaeology Division, Royal Ontario Museum, University of Toronto. Toronto: Ontario Department of Lands and Forests.

[210] 1963. *The Hunting Group–Hunting Territory Complex among the Mistassini Indians.* National Museum of Canada Bulletin:195, Anthropological Series:63. Ottawa: Department of Northern Affairs and National Resources.

*[211] 1964. "The Fur Trade, the Government, and the Central Canadian Indian." *Arctic Anthropology* 2:37–40.

[212]　1965. "Leadership among the Indians of Eastern Subarctic Canada." *Anthropologica* 7:263–84.

[213]　1967. *The Material Culture of the Mistassini.* National Museum of Canada, Bulletin:218, Anthropological Series:80. Ottawa: Department of the Secretary of State.

[214]　1964. "Band Organization among the Indians of Eastern Subarctic Canada." In *Contributions to Anthropology: Band Societies,* ed. David Damas, pp. 21–50. See [142].

[215]　1969. "Natural Environmental-Social Organization–Witchcraft: Cree Versus Ojibwa—a Test Case." In *Contributions to Anthropology: Ecological Essays,* ed. David Damas, pp. 24–39. National Museums of Canada Bulletin:230, Anthropological Series:86. Ottawa: National Museums of Canada.

[216]　1973. *The Quest for Food and Furs, the Mistassini Cree, 1953–1954.* National Museum of Man Publications in Ethnology:5 Ottawa: National Museums of Canada.

[217]　Forthcoming. "History of Ethnological Research in the Shield Subarctic." In *The Subarctic,* ed. June Helm. See [91].

[218]　Rogers, Edward S. and Trudeau, Father John. 1971. "The Indians of the Central Subarctic of

Canada." In *Proceedings of the 38th International Congress of Americanists*, vol. 3, pp. 133–49. See [200].

[219] Rogers, George W. 1971. "Goodbye, Great White Father-Figure." *Anthropologica* (Special Issue: *Pilot Not Commander*, eds. Pat and James Lotz) 13:279–306. See [208].

[220] Ross, Bernard R., Esq. 1867. "The Eastern Tinneh." In *Annual Report for the Year 1866 of the Smithsonian Institution*, pp. 303–11. See [81].

*[221] Russell, Frank. 1898. *Explorations in the Far North, Being the Report of an Expedition under the Auspices of the University of Iowa During the Years 1892, '93 and '94*. Iowa City: University of Iowa.

*[222] Sanders, Douglas Esmond. 1973. *Native People in Areas of Internal National Expansion: Indians and Inuit of Canada*. International Work Group for Indigenous Affairs, Document No. 14. Copenhagen: International Work Group for Indigenous Affairs.

[223] Savishinsky, Joel S. 1974. *The Trail of the Hare: Life and Stress in an Arctic Community*. New York: Gordon and Breach.

[224] Savoie, Donat. 1971. "Bibliographie d'Emile Petitot, Missionaire dans le Nord-Ouest Canadien." *Anthropologica* (Special Issue: *Pilot Not*

Commander, eds. Pat and James Lotz) 13:159–68. See [208].

[225]   Skinner, Alanson. 1911. *Notes on the Eastern Cree and Northern Salteaux.* Anthropological Papers of the American Museum of Natural History:9, pp. 1–177. New York: The Trustees.

Slobodin, Richard.

[226]   1962. *The Band Organization of the Peel River Kutchin.* National Museum of Canada,- Bulletin:179. Ottawa: Department of Northern Affairs and National Resources.

[227]   1966. *Metis of the Mackenzie District.* Ottawa: Research Centre for Anthropology, St. Paul University.

[228]   1969. "Leadership and Participation in a Kutchin Trapping Party." In *Contributions to Anthropology: Band Societies,* ed. David Damas, pp. 56–89. See [142].

[229]   1970. "Kutchin Concepts of Reincarnation." *Western Canadian Journal of Anthropology* (Special Issue: *Athabaskan Studies*) 2:67–79.

[230]   Smith, David Merrill. 1973. *Inkonze: Magico-Religious Beliefs of Contact–Traditional Chipewyan Trading at Fort Resolution, N. W. T., Canada.* National Museum of Man, Mercury Series, Ethnol-

ogy Division Paper:6. Ottawa: National Museums of Canada.

[231] Smith, Derek G. n.d. *The Mackenzie Delta — Domestic Economy of the Native Peoples.* Mackenzie Delta Research Project:3. Ottawa: Northern Co-ordination and Research Centre, Department of Indian Affairs and Northern Development.

[232] Smith, James G. E. 1975. "The Ecological Basis of Chipewyan Socio-Territorial Organization." In *Proceedings; Northern Athabaskan Conference 1971,* ed. A. McFayden Clark, vol. 2, pp. 384 – 461. See [44].

Speck, Frank Gouldsmith.

[233] 1914. *The Double Curve Motive in Northeast Algonkian Art.* Canada Department of Mines, Geological Survey, Memoir:42, Anthropological Series:1. Ottawa: Department of Mines.

[234] 1915. "The Family Hunting Band as the Basis of Algonkian Social Organization." *American Anthropologist* 17:289–305.

*[235] 1935. *Naskapi: The Savage Hunters of the Labrador Peninsula.* Norman: University of Oklahoma Press.

[236] 1937. "Montagnais Art in Birch-Bark: A Circumpolar Trait." *Indian Notes and Monographs* 11:45–157.

[237] Speck, Frank Gouldsmith and Eisley, Loren C. 1942. "Montagnais-Naskapi Bands and Family Hunting Districts of the Central and Southeastern Labrador Peninsula." *Proceedings of the American Pholosophical Society* 85:215–42.

[238] Steward, Julian Haynes 1955. "Variation in Ecological Adaptation: The Carrier Indians." In *Theory of Culture Change, the Methodology of Multilinear Evolution,* by Julian H. Steward, pp. 173-77. Urbana: University of Illinois Press.

*[239] Stoddard, Natalie. 1972. "Some Ethnological Aspects of the Russian Fur Trade." In *People and Pelts,* ed. Malvina Bolus, pp. 39–58. See [192].

[240] Strong, William Duncan. 1929. "Cross-cousin Marriage and the Culture of the Northeastern Algonkian." *American Anthropologist* 31:277–88.

*[241] Sullivan, Robert Jeremiah. 1942. *The T'ena Food Quest.* Catholic University of America Anthropological Series:11. Washington, D.C.: Catholic University of America Press.

[242] Swanton, John Reed. 1952. *The Indian Tribes of North America.* Smithsonian Institution, Bureau of American Ethnology, Bulletin:145. Washington, D.C.: U. S. Government Printing Office.

[243] Teicher, Morton I. 1960. *Windigo Psychosis.* Proceedings of the 1960 Annual Spring Meet-

ing of the American Ethnological Society. Seattle: University of Washington Press.

[244]   Teit, James Alexander. 1956. "Field Notes on the Tahltan and Kaska Indians, 1912–1915." *Anthropologica* 3:39–171.

*[245]   Tetso, John. 1970. *Trapping is My Life.* Toronto: Peter Martin Associates, Ltd.

*[246]   Thompson, David. 1916. *David Thompson's Narrative of his Explorations in Western America 1784–1812,* ed. Joseph Burr Tyrrell. Toronto: The Champlain Society. (Facsimile ed., Greenwood Press, New York, 1968.)

*[247]   Thwaites, Rueben Gold, ed. 1896–1901. "Document XXIII, Le Jeune's Relation, 1634." In *The Jesuit Relations and Allied Documents: Travels and Explorations of the Jesuit Missionaries in New France, 1610–1791,* ed. Rueben G. Thwaites, 73 vols., vol. 6, pp. 91–330 and vol. 7, pp. 5–235. Cleveland: The Burrows Brothers Co.

[248]   Todd, Evelyn. Forthcoming. "Historical Linguistics and Dialect Geography: Algonquian Languages." In *The Subarctic,* ed. June Helm. See [91].

Townsend, Joan B.

[249]   1970. "Tanaina Ethnohistory: An Example of a Method for the Study of Cultural Change." In

Ethnohistory in Southwestern Alasks, ed. Margaret Lantis, pp. 71–102. See [159].

*[250]   1970. "The Tanaina of Southwestern Alaska: An Historical Synopsis." *Western Canadian Journal of Anthropology* (Special Issue: *Athabaskan Studies*) 2:2–16.

[251]   1947. "Journals of 19th Century Russian Priests to the Tanaina: Cook Inlet, Alaska." *Arctic Anthropology* 11:1–30.

[252]   Turner, Lucien McShan. 1894. "Ethnology of the Ungava District, Hudson Bay Territory." Smithsonian Institution, Bureau of Ethnology, *Eleventh Annual Report, 1889–90,* pp. 159–350. Washington, D.C.: U. S. Government Printing Office.

[253]   United States Federal Field Committee for Developmental Planning in Alaska. 1968. *Alaska Natives and the Land.* Anchorage, Alaska: U. S. Government Printing Office.

[254]   United States Senate Report. 1900. *Compilation of Narratives of Explorations in Alaska.* See [199].

VanStone, James W.

[256]   1965. *The Changing Culture of the Snowdrift Chipewyan.* National Museum of Canada, Bulletin:209, Anthropological Series:74. Ottawa: Department of the Secretary of States.

[257] 1970. "An Introduction to Baron F. P. Von Wrangell's Observations on the Eskimos and Indians of Alaska." *Arctic Anthropology* 6:1–4.

*[258] 1974. *Athapaskan Adaptations: Hunters and Fishermen of the Subarctic Forests*. Chicago: Aldine Pub. Co.

*[259] Vaudrin, Bill. 1969. *Tanaina Tales from Alaska*. Norman: University of Oklahoma Press.

[260] Von Wrangell, Ferdinand Petrovich. 1970. "The Inhabitants of the Northwest Coast of America," trans. and ed., James W. VanStone. *Arctic Anthropology* 6:5–20.

[261] *Western Canadian Journal of Anthropology*. 1969– . Edmonton, Alberta: Department of Anthropology, University of Alberta.

*[262] Wheeler, David E. 1914. "The Dog-Rib Indian and His Home." *Bulletin of the Geographical Society of Philadelphia* 12:47–69.

Whymper, Frederick.

[263] 1868. "Russian America, or 'Alaska': the Natives of the Youkon River and Adjacent Country." *Transactions of the Ethnological Society* 7:167–85.

*[264] 1868. *Travel and Adventure in the Territory of Alaska, Formerly Russian America — Now Ceded to the United States — and in Various Other Parts of the North Pacific*. London: J. Murray.

[265] Willey, Gordon Randolph. 1966. *An Introduction to American Archaeology.* 2 vols. Englewood Cliffs, N.J.: Prentice-Hall, Inc. [Volume 1 is germane to Subarctic concerns.]

*[266] Willis, Jane. 1973. *Geniesh: An Indian Girlhood.* Toronto: New Press.

*[267] Wilson, Clifford. 1970. *Campbell of the Yukon.* Toronto: Macmillan of Canada.

Wolfart, H. Christoph.

[268] 1973. "Boundary Maintenance in Algonquian: A Linguistic Study of Island Lake, Manitoba." *American Anthropologist* 75:1305–23.

[269] 1973. "The Current State of Cree Language Studies." *Western Canadian Journal of Anthropology* 3:38–35.

[270] Wolfart, H. Christoph and Carroll, Janet F. 1973. *Meet Cree: A Practical Guide to the Cree Language.* Edmonton: University of Alberta Press.

[271] Workman, Karen W. 1972. *Alaskan Archaeology: A Bibliography.* Miscellaneous Publications, History and Archaeology Series:1. Anchorage: Alaska Division of Parks.

[272] Wright, J. V. Forthcoming. "The Prehistory of the Shield." In *The Subarctic,* ed. June Helm. See [91].

The Newberry Library
Center for the History of the American Indian

Director: Francis Jennings

Established in 1972 by the Newberry Library, in conjunction with the Committee on Institutional Cooperation of eleven midwestern universities, the Center makes the resources of one of America's foremost research libraries in the Humanities available to those interested in improving the quality and effectiveness of teaching American Indian history. The Newberry's collections include some 100,000 volumes on the history of the American Indian and offer specialized resources for studying historical aspects of Indian–White relations and Indian linguistics. The Center also assists Native Americans engaged in writing tribal histories and developing educational materials.

ADVISORY COMMITTEE

Chairman: D'Arcy McNickle